CHORONZON

THE OFFICIAL JOURNAL OF MARTINET PRESS

Volume III

ISBN 978-0-9997680-0-6

Edited by Erica Frevel

Cover art by Konstantyn Kopacz of Warhead Art

Back cover quote attributed to Erichthro's necrosophic incantation found in
Lucan's Epic Pharsalia, Book VI

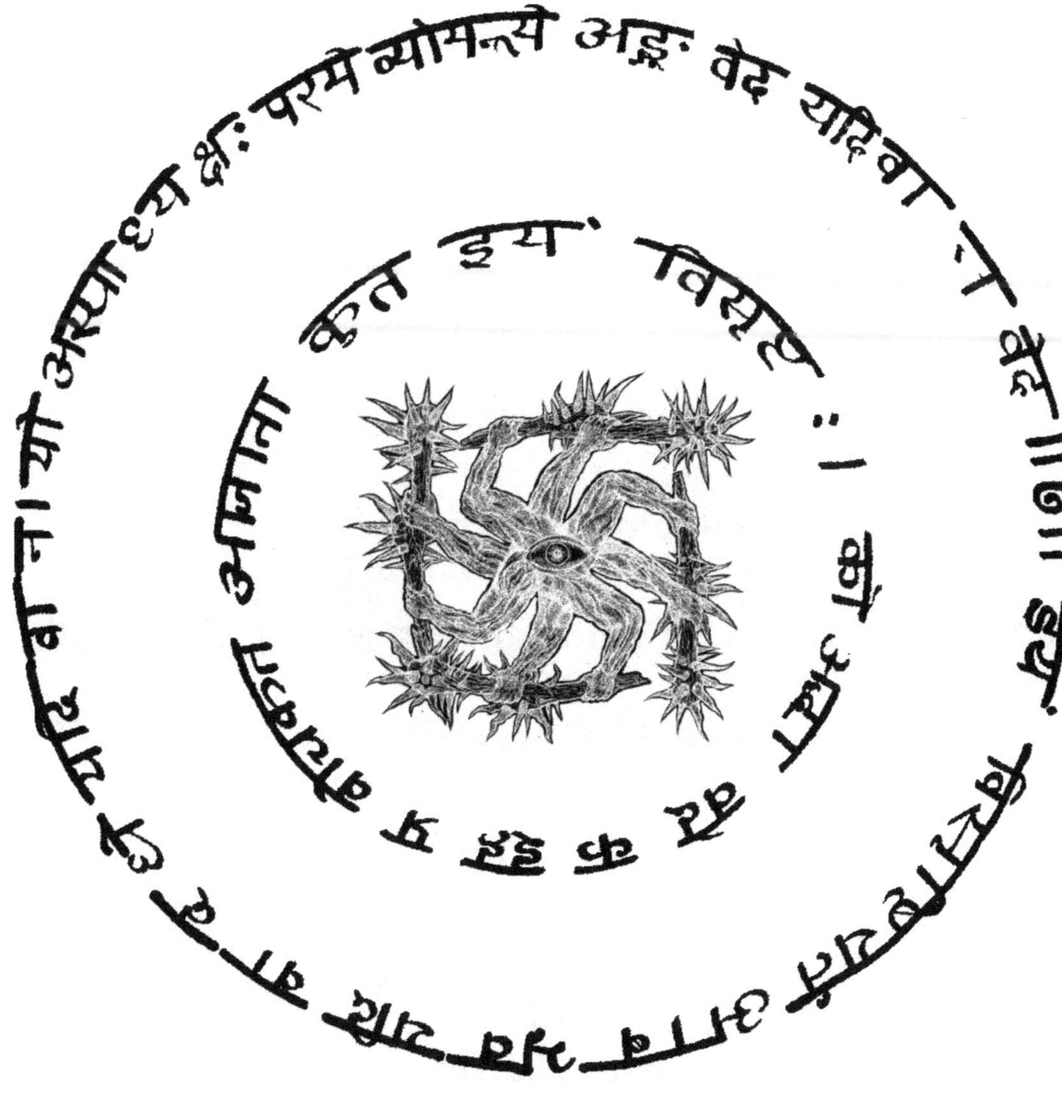

यो अस्याध्यक्षः परमे व्योमन्त्सो अङ्गः वेद यदि वा न वेद ॥७॥
अजाता कुत इयं विसृष्टिः ।

Contents

From the desk of the Editor:

It is my profound pleasure to introduce to you the third installment of Choronzon from the auspices of Martinet Press. The journal you hold in your hands contains artwork, oftentimes containing blood, that has been used by the artists as portals to the other side. Every artist is also an active occultist in their chosen discipline, whether it be hermetic or within their order. Take these pages, cut them out with razors, saturate in blood and use them as altar pieces to call the darkness into your heart and mind. As I write this, in the first days of Saturnalia, I implore you to become a permanent agent of Chaos.

Disruption and corruption, thou art our Father.

It is a great honor to become both editor and contributor for this and future volumes. As many of you may know, I am first and foremost an agent of the Abyss. My personal artistic work has been featured in the first two volumes of Choronzon. Everything I produce, whether it be paintings, collages or written word has the sole purpose of bringing the Abyss into the material realm. It is a calling which I have been acting upon for my entire life (albeit unbeknownst to myself at times). I continue to saturate the earthly plane with the energy of the other side as editor of this journal. Thank you to the writers, artists and black occultists who have joined me in this calling and entrust me with their work to include in this volume. Our efforts are not in vain; there are more and more of us each day who are able to see past the mundane and into the horrifying alien agenda of the Void through Satanic ritual practice. Those whose work could not fit into this volume are encouraged to submit more of their material in the upcoming volumes.

As Satanists, it is our duty to carry our nightmarish banners into the new aeon. Despite our myriad sinister traditions, we all have one goal: to master our spiritual evolution to become a beacon of evil... to become a living, breathing representative of Satan while here on Earth. In hiding and in broad daylight, we strive to manipulate this world with the blackest of magick until it is a suitable environment for our dark gods. The unjust rule of the Nazarene will not survive this new world.

If you hear ITS grinding, sadistic voice of metallic static reverberate in your inner most skull, you know what must be done.

The future is delightfully bleak and the time is ours, my brothers and sisters.

Satanas Vobiscum

666

𝕷𝖔𝖗𝖉 𝕶𝖗𝖎𝖘𝖍𝖓𝖆

Collage, ink and blood on board
Erica Frevel
From the private collection of ToB

Vindex

In traditional demonology, Lucifer is known as the Emperor of Hell, lord of all demons. In dark magic Medieval books, Lucifer is described as the biggest one in power among all the devils.

Not only does he have devilish and infernal feature but also a pure gnostic self. It is important to observe that "Lucifer" is just a generic term used as an adjective for entities, not a proper name as thought. Lucifer can be understood as "the one who brings light", "the light carrier", "the lord of spiritual enlightenment", so, it's possible to affirm that many spiritual beings, dark gods and deities around the world have luciferic characteristics.

In the beliefs of Traditional Satanism, both Lucifer and Satan are names for chaotic, sinister and non-causal spiritual forces coming from Dark Gods, an intangible idea for mere mental understanding. Anyway, exoterically speaking, those names fit well for antinomian, rebel, dark, sinister nature representation of those Dark Gods who are the Bestial Chaos Beginning themselves.

In Satanic tradition, Satan is shown as a chaotic, transcendental, non causal, dark god, having violent instincts of creation and destruction. It's perceptible the dark alchemy principle inside Satanic Mysteries.

In India, Lord Krishna is represented by a chaotic, destructive and creative transcendental non-causal dark blue God, being sinister and violent many times. Lord Krishna commits violent acts such as murder and destruction, as luxury acts.

According to The Dark Tradition, there are many similarities between Lord Krishna and Satanic essences. According to Bhagavad Gita, Lord Krishna says that among his devils, he is the greatest one. Vedic literature also has many demons and obscure demigods subjecting themselves to him. In this aspect, Lord Krishna is seen as a supreme being on the Infernal Cosmic Hierarchy as so does Lucifer in the Medieval Black Magic Tradition.

CHORONZON III

Lord Krishna presents a luciferic gnostic ethos, coming to Earth from time to time to teach the transcendental truth for the human beings bringing enlightenment and knowledge as well, as Lucifer and Prometheus, remembering the superiority of the spirit over the material which is the core precept of Gnostic Currents.

Besides that, Krishna is beyond Brahma and before Brahma, as Satan is beyond Ayin manifestations and before Ayin manifestations as the three chaotic levels: pre-cosmic, cosmic and anti- cosmic. In this context, Krishna can be compared with Satan in Chaos Gnosticism.

As Vindex, and assuming the Vindex Krishna role, Krishna promises to kill the weaker ones and bring the New Aeon for the strongest ones through genocide. The Lord Kalki avatar (which is the Vindex itself) will make a huge bloodshed in honor of Lord Visnu (Purushamedha). Washing the Earth with unfaithful and weak blood will bring a New Aeon belonging to the strongest ones, the numinous, the new elite called obscure aristocracy.

Lord Krishna can represent all the obscure gods from the dark traditions himself; as death gobbling life and as eternal life after death. Gnostic transcendence can be achieved by doing maha-mantra at least 16 japamalas times everyday as a fervent devotional act and as black mysticism.

Sing maha-mantra and join the Vindex Army praying for ruthless and massive execution by Lord Kalki's sword, offering weak blood to Lord Krishna who is the Vindex itself. May it bring a new world sinister order, a place where only the strong devotees will survive!

hare krishna!

X.ᵉ INCARNATION DE VICHENOU
sous la forme d'un Cheval.

Illustration of Lord Sri Kalki
"Voyage aux Indes orientales et à la Chine"
Pierre Sonnerat, 1782

Devouring the Cosmos
Acrylic on canvas
Barry James Lent

Suffering in Eternity
Acrylic on canvas
Barry James Lent

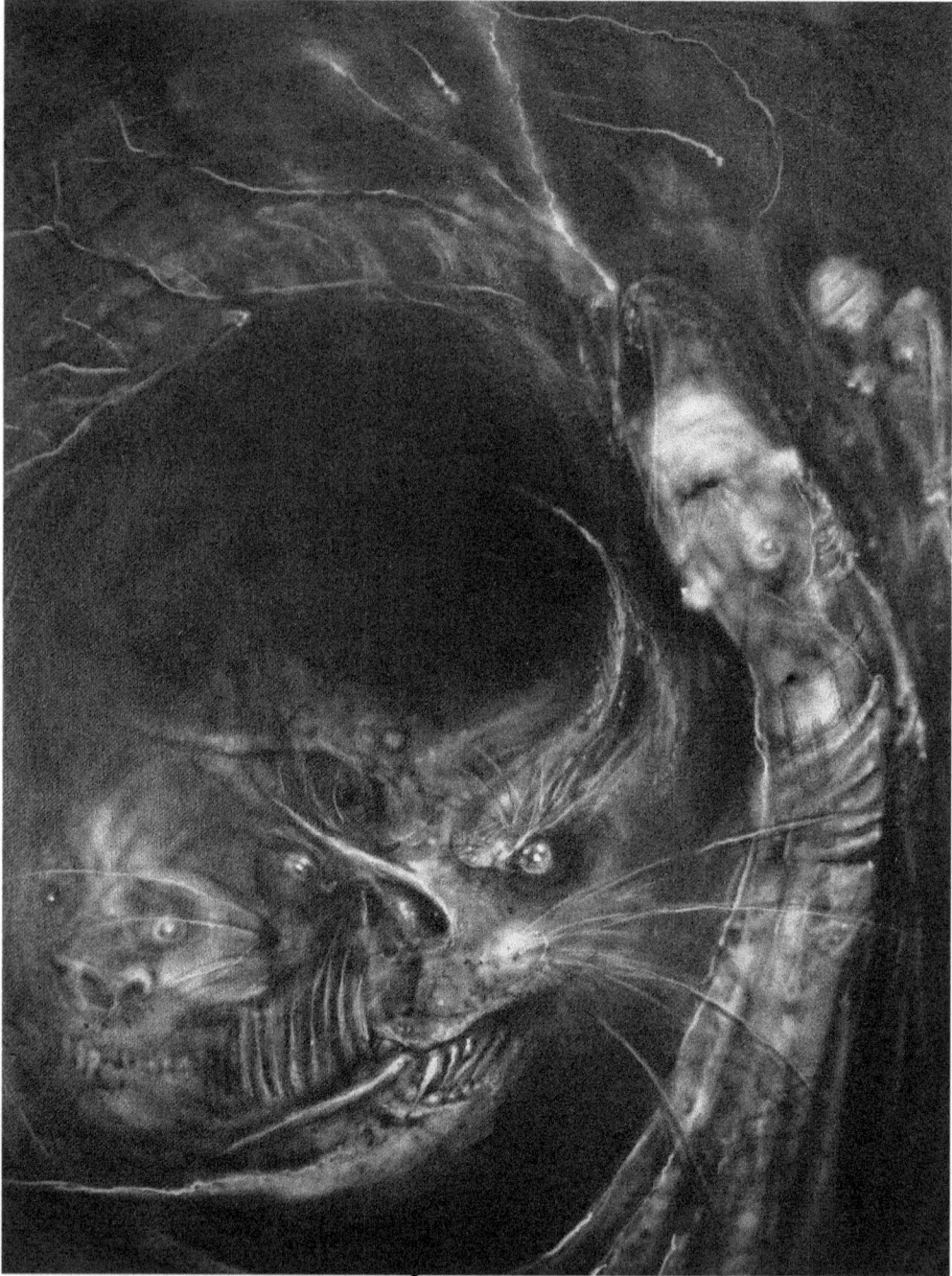

The Dark Recess
Acrylic on canvas
Barry James Lent

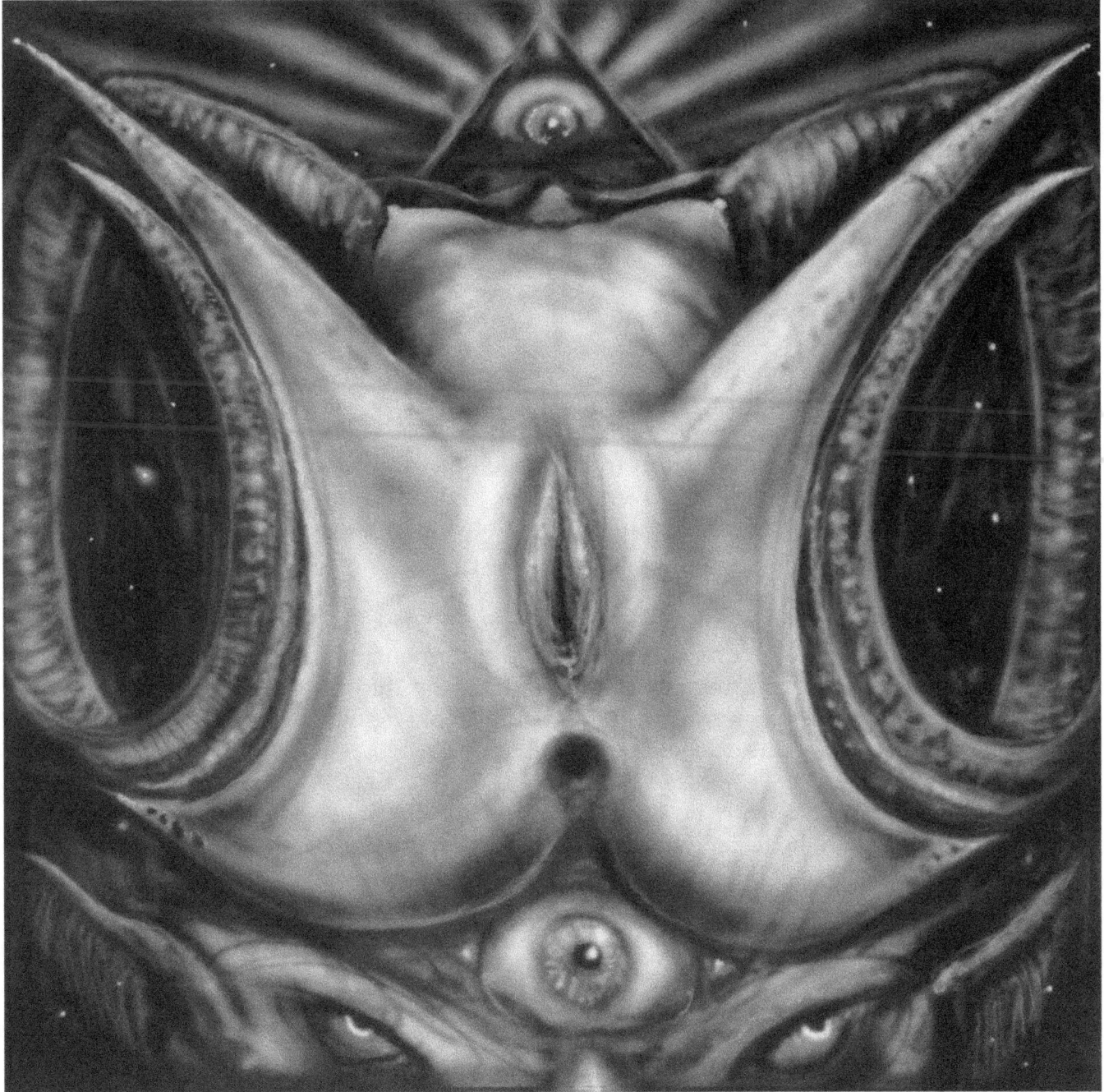

𝕭abalon

Acrylic on canvas
Barry James Lent

𝔏era's Torment

Aubrey Wood Basnight

Part 8

There was only one door to the street from his corridor of the hotel - namely the main entrance out past the lobby - where, even from this present vantage, he could tell that the protest continued. So-called protest, Max considered now. Was the purpose of the obstruction in front of the hotel to block him from exit or to provide a degree of cover - a diversion - for him being renditioned? One thing was for sure - they had let him in, but they obviously did not intend on letting him out.

He rushed into a pair of clothes, a faded brown BDU jacket and matching EMC tactical trousers, well-worn. He wrapped the torment in the shirt that he had been wearing earlier in the day and stuffed it deep into his only other piece of luggage besides his leather satchel - a uni-style bookbag which he strapped to his bag before throwing the satchel over his shoulder.

Scanning the room quickly he saw that nothing discernible had been left behind. For good measure he fastened all security locks on the door and then shoved the top of the desk chair underneath the handle.

Max opened the window that led to the outside - the light now beginning to exude that nauseating glow, not dissimilar to that which emanated from the torment only a few minutes early, that typified the desert during pre-twilight. The sun appeared like a hazy malignant orb in the sky - its contours and features obscured by high-riding parched sands riding the wind currents and the clinging smog of unregulated industry.

No interior screen was present to keep out the desert gnats, nor were the security of the establishment's temporary inhabitants considered crucial enough to warrant bars on the window - the latter for which Max was extremely thankful for at this particular point.

Exiting the window, large enough, was no problem as his room was situated, as were all the others, on ground floor. The wings of the corridor stretched out from the main lobby in a slightly sideward fashion so that he would not be directly perpendicular with the protesters and assorted others outside - though he would potentially be visible to those on the outskirts of their number.

Despite this he would assume that his room was being watched - but he bargained that the surveillance would be heavier on the outside than the inside. A man climbing out of a window, even one conveniently situated, was a strange sight anywhere one might be however he trusted that the pedestrians would mind their own business - at least that is if they were not on the payroll of those who were attempting his detention.

Throwing one leg over the sill and then the other Max was out. He turned a two o'clock position headed in the opposite direction of the hotel over the street and was off at a quick pace - sometimes jogging through the traffic snaking across the boulevard - not looking behind him in case surveillance was on him.

Horns honked as he blockaded the forward motion of a small truck overloaded with crates for the market, a rickety Datsun with wheels nearly flattened by the back-end preponderance. He kept his head down and moved forward and the traffic once again began moving forward, ever so slowly, as impatient couriers and commuters on dirt bikes and other small motorcycles sliced their way down the middle of the lanes between larger traffic.

Max found an alley which seemed less travelled, darkened by rusted sheet metal roofing and a few precarious catwalks which blocked those below from the sun and the rare rainfall. An old man knelt against the wall of the soot-black wall behind which once resided a small tannery - long since closed. The old man smiled dementedly, drawing on a bent and bedraggled cigarette. Eastern-European import? Max thought to himself, sniffing and smiling in return. He made for the relative cover of the alley post-haste.

If his calculations were correct this alley would connect him to the next major road which led perpendicular to the one in which his hotel was located on. He would have to find a way out of the city from there.

The kingdom had only one major international airport and in fact only a few airports in general - though there was several military bases and at least one that serviced international flights further to the south but only for private jets and other contracted transport. That would have been the entry point for the people who were tracking him from abroad - that or the military bases, though the latter might be a bit too overt for their purposes, though it all depended if what they were doing here was being done with the concurrence of the resident intelligence forces or not. Max had his doubts. The uniformed police he saw back at the entrance of the hotel as well as prior to the procession could be on anybody's payroll - perhaps themselves agents and as such technically traitors to their own government - and as such, capable of anything.

Max bisected his way through a few loitering street people as he entered the mouth of the alleyway - their eyes diverting from each other briefly in assessment for potential exploitation yet only briefly - his evident mania and sense of mission indicating that targeting him, albeit foreign as he obviously was, would be too much trouble all things considered.

Taking the narrow passage at a commando's gait, Max was thankful for the relative lack of inhabitants - indicating to him instinctually that he had chosen the correct passage toward the secondary main road ahead which would provide the first leg in his escape route. The shade from above was welcome, adding if only in a cosmetic sense to his desire for covert movement - though even within the intermittent shade he could tell that the late-afternoon was dwindling minute by minute toward genuine twilight.

The shadows darkened around him and he could feel a resurgence of the dissociation he felt earlier when dealing with the torment directly. Situated deep within the pack upon which he shouldered, he could tell that the eldritch item was transmitting to him in vague yet distinct telepathic fashion palpable prompts for his escape - as if the torment was desirous of him making a successful escape from the individuals and hostile forces which sought to interdict him along the way. For this he was thankful and furthermore, took as a proof positive that his destiny and that of the torment were interlocked at this moment in time.

A few minutes only passed before he was clear of the alleyway and into the secondary main road running parallel to his former hotel. No signs of surveillance were seen - indicating that perhaps both opposing intelligence agencies - including nefarious operatives acting on behalf of the dealer and ancillary parties - were operating on skeleton crews themselves. The thought brought a brief emotive response akin to smugness within his mind, though not so much that it would cloud his judgement. Success would be measured in this particular leg of his journey according to how quickly - and how successfully - he was able to get himself out of the country. Anywhere, everywhere - though the more obscure the better - better than here, out from the scent of the onward hunt.

Careening across the intersection toward the walkway on the other side of the street a filament of a forward plan began to germinate in Max's mind. He knew a place where he could take refuge for the longterm - even if his North American domiciles had been compromised at this point, which he had every reason to believe that they were.

But what of the problem if they had put a hold on his passport? And restrictions on transportable items, the strictures which had been considerably tightened by all international flights who took their cues, even peripherally, from the dictates of the federal aviation administration.

He put his faith in the torment. If the torment had led him this far in his quest for consummation with the powers that dwelt within - if the torment had moved him physically across continents and within situations of imminent danger repeatedly, the most prominent example being in the here and now, then it would get him to safe haven.

Part 9

After crossing the intersection Max restrained his pace to a slow, natural gait, walking block after block and keeping himself on the main road as twilight advanced along with his progress to the full night coverage of early evening.

The direction he was taking was leading him out of the more seedy areas of the city where most of his business had taken place and toward more habitable climes which were the more usual destinations of foreign travellers. Both parties that had been conducting surveillance on him, which he believed he had now foiled, at least for a time, would also have access to these more affluent areas - though renditioning him here would be much more difficult, especially if the local authorities were not in on the game.

His plan had gone from a filament of strategy only into full-flower during the time that he had been walking, around an hour and a half now and it was now time to begin putting it into motion.

The street was now bereft of the more squalid vendor stalls, though there were still a few food and drink vendors loitering here and there. In contrast to the area in which he had been prior there were actually some decent looking restaurants and even some night-clubs, outside of the latter which crowded the up and coming members of the young professional class, the venue catering to their metropolitan tastes and aspirations, with a smattering of smart and attractive foreign nationals in the mix as well.

Max suddenly was aware of the fact that he was famished and that particularly moment in time he wanted nothing more than to walk himself into the best of the restaurants along the strand, rest his aching muscles in a luxuriant leather cushioned booth and recover physically and mentally with a stiff drink and the largest steak he could order. Not yet however, he thought somewhat morbidly - though he did slake his thirst and immediate hunger with a extremely black coffee and a kebab, pleasantly charred, which he consumed while leaning against the corner of a building, well within the shadows and not visible from the passing traffic.

He scanned the various cars parked several yards down from where he stood - the uniformed, readily identifiable cabs - their rate system and telephone of owning company and/or owner-operators painted on the side or affixed in large commercially printed magnets. Amidst them the more marginal privately run commuters - cheap fleet cars with alert looking, usually younger drivers ready to negotiate fare schedules with their clients for a cut of the business. At the end of the line he could see a battered mini-van, with an exterior body that showed it was very well travelled indeed, reminding him of a similar model in similar condition which he had seen (and subsequently ridden in) years ago in a bombed-out neighbourhood of Beirut. Just suitable.

Max drained the last dregs of coffee from his paper cup before squatting and placing it on the ground next to the wall and inserting the kebab skewer - cleaned of meat - leaning against its side, as there were no visible trash receptacles visible in the immediate vicinity. Stepping into the light of the sidewalk yet staying as far over toward the shadows as possible Max made his way at a leisurely pace toward the mini-van, one hand reaching into his side pocket as he did so.

Reaching the driver's side window, a stout man most definitely of Indian birth, very dark complexion - every inch a Dravidian - a Keralite or Tamilan - looked back at Max with a tentative smile beneath thick black mustache, nearly a

13

handlebar - the expectancy of custom. Max smiled in return, much wider, before extending his arm and displaying a goodly stack of U.S. dollars, tapping the wad against window jam but keeping his hand cupped so that it would not be readily viewable should someone be passing from the walk behind him. The cabman's tentative smile turned genuine at this universal gesture and he beckoned with his head. "Come, come!" he said in an accent with little or no regional inflection. The driver reached back and popped the lock on the backseat roller door and Max climbed in, dropping the back containing the torment between his feet, slammed the door behind him and leaned back against the welcome cushion of the aging bench seat. The engine engaged and the van with passenger slid out into the medium traffic - headed away from the city.

Part 10

His driver, as was revealed during the midst of casual conversation along the drive, was in fact a Tamilan and of Sri Lankan birth. The driver's family had emigrated from the Jaffna peninsula during a period in the early nineteen-nineties when the so-called civil conflict between the inhabitants of the region and the government to the south had been at a lull, when he was only a child. Pottu Amman was his name, as he told Max, which made Max smile silently from the backseat - as he knew that this was a pseudonym - a pseudonym of another, no less, an intelligence chief from the insurrection years later when the driver would have been at a particularly impressionable age and inhabiting a particularly volatile and fanatic climate amongst the Tamil Sri Lankan emigre community. The name in passable translation denoted "blood tilak" - the latter designating a religious facial marking, the former obvious - combined being somewhat blasphemous and quite completely revolutionary in import.

Max and Pottu drove and it was sooner than Max had anticipated that they were beyond the city - the lights of the desert metropolis shining dimly in the rear-view mirrors of the van and the grime-encrusted headlight covers illuminating a passably driveable but very remote stretch of highway that would lead them in an hour or two to the border crossing, shortly past which was Max's intended destination.

Pottu had no problems with accepting a fare beyond his locale, his choice of vehicle and demeanour being a positive signal which all seasoned international and domestic travellers would recognize as being indicative of willing to take a risk if the price was right. He had lived with his family after they had immigrated abroad - his memories of his native Jaffna now only faded visions of fertile jungle and a hellishly hot coastline, sometimes interspersed with the even more hellish aerial bombardments from governmental military and the dire disappearances of the fathers of his friends and some of his own cousins and uncles in the unmarked black vans that would perform snatch-and-grab operations even during the daylight hours - many of those taken never to be seen again.

It was with a sense of dark irony then that Pottu himself had found himself driving a van for his sustenance many years later - with those unforgettable images from his childhood in the back of his mind, sometimes witnessed from the second story window of the colonial building which was the setting of his grammar school, he and his classmates gathered at the ancient pane windows exclamating before their teacher would loudly shuttle them back into their seats - suffuse with protestations in order to foster the pretense of normality for the children but with cold dread sweat dripping down their backs wondering who amongst their neighbours might have been taken and if they themselves might be next in line.

While Pottu's family had settled - if settled could be the proper word - in the United Arab Emirates, his father, a trained engineer with a university diploma, quickly gaining a job working on some of the enormous pipelines criss-crossing the region - Pottu himself had decided to move further afield once in his late teens. Now nearing the cusp of thirty, he had resided in North Africa for some years and carved out for himself a marginal yet profitable niche for his standards.

Max's intentions once across the border were simple. He had provided Pottu enough currency to bribe the border officials without much ado and Pottu himself had assured him that he had made a similar trip many times before for many sundry clients - and, as Max thought, probably for much less than he himself had paid up front. But that had been his prerogative - he knew that there were forces working against him, with resources much larger than he himself possessed - a fact that he had not divulged to his driver but which Pottu probably guessed, though probably not to what extent. Max had given Pottu an ample amount of cash to work with and with the understanding that the remainder - after his bribing the border guards - would constitute his recompensation for the journey. With that knowledge firmly in mind, Pottu intended to bargain the hired security down to the least passable sum for entry into their country. As he would be arriving at the border crossing late, they would have the younger men on guard and with a few bottles of foreign whisky in the boot kept on hand for just such occasions (bootleg mind you, labels sometime lie - though the deception would be sufficient for the Islamic palate, per prior experience) Pottu had every faith that the crossing would be effected with minimal damage to his incipient profit margin.

Max stared from the sideward mirror out into the vast desert landscape surrounding him. An unsettled peace had come upon him in the half-hour or so since he had left the city - the lack of any headlights following them from the distance an indicator that he had more than likely lost his tail even as soon as exiting the hotel many hours ago. This strengthened his belief that the torment was in control of the situation - from a foul, occult vantage of influence - for his escape had been too easy, too effortless against forces that were clearly most professional in orientation. The thought that the torment had arranged his safe-passage even this far was humbling to him, for though his fanaticism waxed strong he could only imagine the sort of sacrifices undertaken by those who bore the object before him. But the time for more severe sacrifices would, as the case may be, lay upon the horizon and - for those to be effected - he needed to be out of harm's way, at least in the immediate sense. Again, the harm, to come later, most assuredly.

The flat alien landscapes passed by at a rapid rate - the stretch of the open road and Max's ample fee to the driver facilitating a median speed bordering on the reckless. Less than a mile beyond upon either side the landscape began to shift into shimmering dunes, hot winds throwing sand in small cyclones and eddies amidst a terrain which meant death to human life and was only livable for the most sturdy of entities and even for them survival was not an easy thing. Beyond that, ahead of them and to the north, insane and eldritch mountain ranges visible far in the distance - twinkling with the greenish light of hallucination and the sadistic fervour of well-entrenched military installations - these marking the border from here into the other through which Max sought a dangerous passage.

With the thoughts of these real-time images within his mind Max considered, his driver having gone silent for sometime now, amidst his own immediate concerns and formulating the stratagems which would take them across shortly, what sort of entities existed in the environs in which he now found himself - so full of not only potential for devastating, exoteric acts but in fact profuse with the sort of ultra-violence, catastrophe and terror only known through a glass darkly by the soft and civilized inhabitants of the lands from which Max himself came and which, despite his myriad travels abroad, still marked him as a civilian - and observer only - to the darkness, not incipient, but manifest, which exhibited itself in regions still obscure to western man.

One thing he did know - and this beyond the shadow of a doubt - is that he was the bearer of the torment. A bearer of something so far beyond the consciousness of those who bore pretense about their adeptship in the black arts - what to speak of the man on the street - that anything, anything could happen. He knew that his hubris was probably part of the game - something that everyone that had come before him in similar circumstance, in possession of the amulet bearing a reputation blacker than black, had probably felt before. Yes, each one of them thought that they possessed the fanaticism that no other had possessed - that the alchemical juxtaposition of themselves and the frightful demonnness that lived within the torment, in an existence eternal, would provide that elusive key toward unlocking a global harvest the likes which none had ever seen.

THE CROSSING

Part 11

His mind a tumult of thoughts of the destiny which awaited him - a destiny which existed in a precarious balance of conflicting forces surrounding him and even moreso the torment - Max had fallen into a fitful sleep as Pottu drove silently and uneventfully those last hundred miles toward the border crossing.

All was quiet as they made their way through the harsh desert landscape, excepting the rumble of the road itself - surprisingly subdued even with the stiffness of the tires, the very ailing suspension of the van and the grit and small rocks which regularly blew in from the wilderness on either side of the track.

Max dreamed uneasy dreams as the van drove on ever closer toward those sickening mountains amidst their unnatural illumination.

He saw himself in a bleak forest - humid and damp in a coldness which bore a harsh chemical scent upon the air, a thick ground fog surrounding an area hermetically enclosed against the sky and anything else which might be surrounding by thick and drooping trees, branches and trunks twisted and leaves too green, creating a canopy through which only the most meagre light shone.

CHORONZON III

In this foreign atmosphere Max sat naked upon a slick greyish rock which stood in a pool of mirky water, the atmospheric climate and the sense of palpable foreboding creating a cold sweat upon his body, making him shiver involuntarily. In his dream a sense of overwhelming anxiety assaulted him - the torment! He had lost it, it was no longer in his possession. His bearings - and the amulet for which he had poured his life these last many months - were both gone. Gone then, a reason for his continued existence. A sense of doom assailed him.

From one of the copses of trees beyond the pool he saw the rustling of leaves, the tinkling of ankle bells and the sound of girlish laughter.

Could it be? Was it her?

The flicker of hope changed his consciousness immediately and he knew that he must investigate the sound.

He endeavoured to raise himself from the rock and to cross the pool toward the edge of the surrounding forest from which the sign of life had emanated however as he took the second step into the knee-deep water he felt himself being inextricably drawn backwards - his movements going in reverse even as his will and body moved forward and then he found himself once again seated upon the rock.

Lips drawn back in an involuntary sneer Max attempted again but this time it was harder still - he was only able to barely dismount the rock and step a foot into the cold murky water before his muscles seized as his body came under remote control being drawn back to his position of bondage. A groan escaped him as the effort had the cumulative effect of a great deal of strenuous exercise concentrated into a few moments of time. His body stressed and tightened and the more he fought against the outside control the more strict the control until he was effectively immobilized.

Overhead, the canopy of trees began to part outward, the limbs of the trees which appeared more and more to be possessed of an evil energy in the sparse light creaking loudly as they did so, exposing an iron firmament covered over with dark greyish-black and fastly moving clouds.

Again, barely perceptible now, came the slight movement from the edge of the treeline and the tinkling of bells, again, the girlish laughter. The laughter was tinged with a sinister edge now however - purposeful - for the entity desired to let him know that it was she who was controlling his bondage, she who held him against the rock - her will dominating his own and through that hideous will, his own physicality.

The canopy of trees now realigned the movement above him stopped and he could hear the sound of hurricane-force winds whipping overhead - though the air within the clearing felt stale, dead, oppressive.

Max felt a palpable sense that he was being bled of energy - as if both the clouds above, the evil trees surrounding him, the fog, the foul water - all had effectively coalesced in some vampiric conspiracy to destroy what lived within him, whatever pathetic energy that he might now possess he thought with some nihilism, so as to add to the lifeforce which lived within them. Beyond that even it could simply be play for entities which had little concern with human life - his discomfiture a side-effect to which they were neither aware nor concerned with and continuing along this line of reasoning their actions all sadism on their part, with no real need at all other than to relish his suffering through senses that were markedly alien to his own.

The sound of the winds above him increased and craning his neck painfully upward at the tumult he could ascertain that the clouds were filled with electrical charge - white lighting strikes erupting at an unnatural rate inside the blackish clouds which now flew by at a rate which transgressed all natural phenomena. The sense of utter displacement - of being in an utterly non-human atmosphere, a foul holding planet in a black site within interdimensional space - was so overwhelming that nausea set on. His body yearned to vomit, to excrete automatically from whatever orifice in the face of abject terror. Yet, the vampirized weakening and induced paralysis of his body did not allow it - causing the bile to rise yet not able to be expunged, the poisons within his blood only increasing with no avenue of escape, no hope of cleansing purge.

Once again the copse of trees across the fetid pool rustled but this time the trees parted - not by any human hand but by themselves, by telepathic command, just as the canopy above had moved earlier but in microcosm. Through this rent - this green archway beyond which could only be seen an impenetrable area of complete and utter darkness - she came. Dressed in black silken garments and headdress, reddish leather straps bearing small bells on her ankles which tinkled with each prancing step, she moved forward out of the darkness a few steps only before stopping. Arms crossed over her chest in a posture of haughtiness she gazed toward his hapless figure - grinning so wide that it appeared almost a painful posture to hold - milky white teeth exposed inside a mouth stretched thin, reddish lips the colour of fresh meat.

She was the picture of the girl that we had seen in the procession earlier in the day but older by several years - fourteen, maybe fifteen. The sense of mania and violence had increased ten-fold in her visage in comparison to what had only intimated earlier despite her gory entourage. And as to age - he could not be sure not simply because that her figure was within an inhabitation that was well beyond the earthly but trebled in the fact that she herself seemed to be commanding all that occurred within down to the most minute feature which Max, in his strictured state, counted himself.

The lightning flashing above him began to illuminate the forest grove which gradually grew darker and darker until only that light from above from the bursts of electric charge within the swiftly moving clouds remained - creating a schizophrenic situation of bursts of clear vision amid lulls of blank darkness. In that light the girl's features began to transform into something more sinister in visage - the lightning flashes revealing her face to his frozen gaze revealing a countenance that had become pale, undead even, suffused with a cold sweat. As her eyes grew darker and more intent upon him Max felt his own eyes closing against their will.

Then - in his mind's eye - he saw her face alone, larger than life as if splashed across a cinemascape - her eyes also closing as she began to laugh with abject abandon, her head rocking backward in insane mirth even more dreadful than before. He saw the blackish clouds begin to surround her all around now, almost minute in comparison with her figure, for she was now a giantess - the extent of her potency and her absolute control over the elements and himself, recklessly wielded, now set in stark relief. It was at this moment that his tongue finally loosened and he began to scream.

Husere Grav

Ritual collage and blood on paper
In support of occulstist of Husere Grav
Vladimír Vácovský

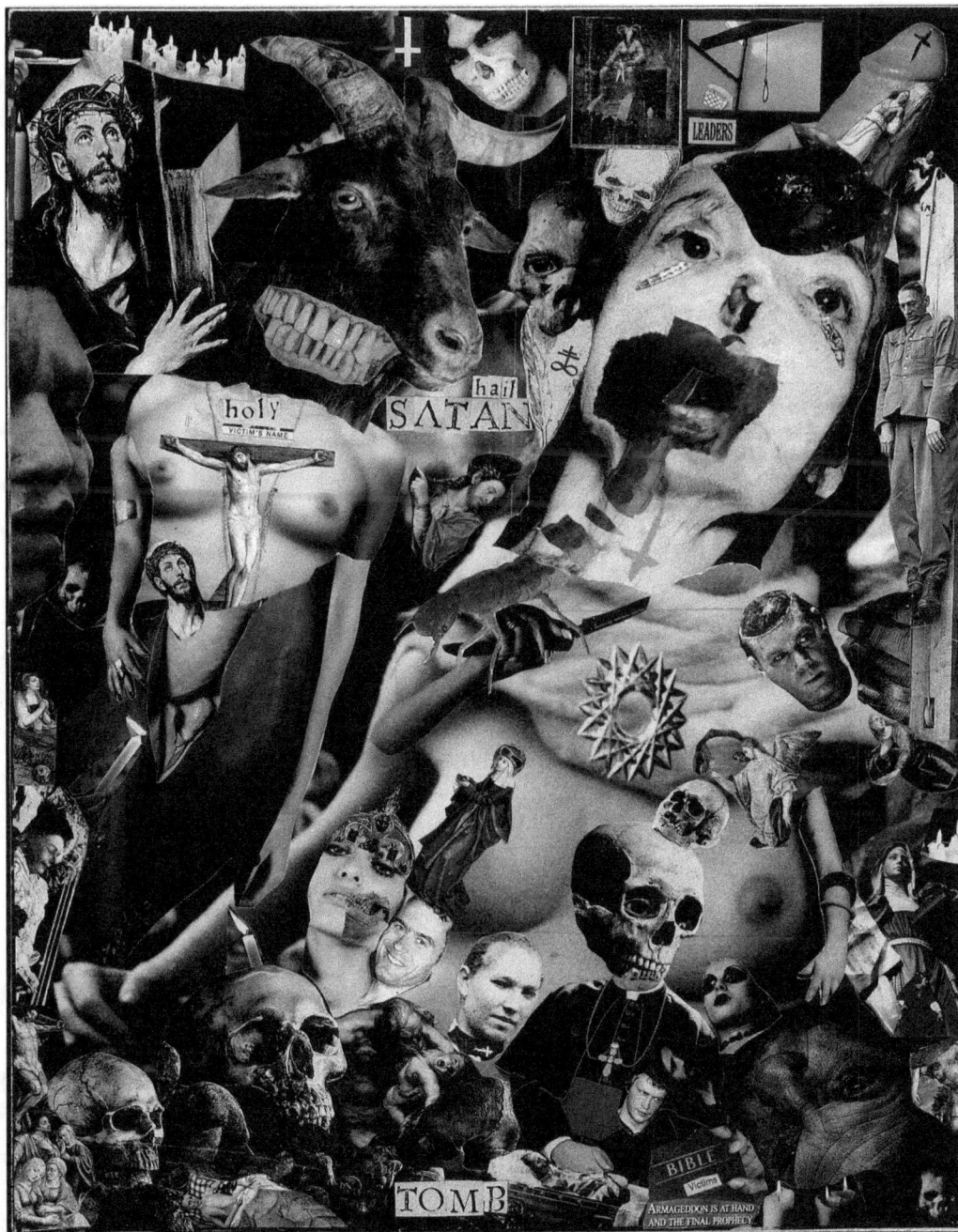

Hail Satan

Ritual collage and blood on paper
In support of occultists of T.O.M.B.
Vladimír Vácovský

Dreadlords

Ritual collage and blood on paper
In support of occultists of Dreadlords
Vladimír Vácovský

CHORONZON III

𝔇atura 𝔉lower
Ink on paper
Chapel of Astaroth

Aspects of Datura Within the Sphere of Nahemoth

Frater Terminus

Within Qlipothic praxis it is known that the initiator of the first Gate of Hell is Nahema/Naamah. From this first gate one is expected to gain the blessings of the five accused nations, the Nephilim, Geburim, Raphaim, Anakim, and Amalekim. The various tribes and spirits hold many connections to Ancient kings and spirits aligned with a satanic praxis i.e. those opposed to the thoughtful side of divinity who are ever striving to tear down and hinder the force of creation. Yet to gain these blessings one must draw the attention of Maiden Lilith (Nahemah) and her flesh and blood manifestation, Naamah, descendant of Cain. Naamah is known within Hebrew and Gnostic scripture to be the seducer of many a man and spirit, namely Azazel. Yet when approaching her she is shrouded in as much darkness and shadow as those leading further into the tree of death. Where should one begin? The present author can only give evidence of what he has encountered within his ritual praxis and experimentation.

The experiment in question is the use of the spirit and essence within the plant Datura as a shamanic guide unto the underworld. It is no secret that Datura is a mighty and terrifying spirit but how does one approach her, let alone make sense of the visions within a scrying mirror and dreams? Strangely enough, the story of this spirit, Datura- Nahemah, not only extends to the ancient Sumerians, the Hebrews but interestingly enough the Aztecs as well.

Briefly explained, according to Lawrence Gardner author of Genesis of the Grail Kings and various other sources : The Annunaki, Enlil took a wife Ninlil. From them gave birth to Nanna-sin the future moon god. As punishment for this, Enlil was sent to the underworld. Upon reaching the Underworld Ninlil disguised her-self as a gatekeeper and seduced Enlil once more to give birth to the god of death Nergal. Gardner goes on to state the Union of the current ruler of the underworld, Erish-Kigal and Nergal could be the progenitors of Lillith. Yet it is interesting to note that upon the Death of Ninlil she was elevated to being a goddess of the wind, practitioners within Satanic current need not have this significance explained. It is of the current authors personal understanding that Ninlil, Lilith, Erish-kigal and Naamah are the same spirit and essence undergoing various changes, reflecting their Chaotic/Chthonic essence.

I obtained a good portion of Datura and after its obtainment performed a ritual invocation of her night side spirit according to Current 182 tradition that I have been practicing for almost 2 years. Within that time I have cared for and grew a Blackthorn plant to be my main helper spirit within this Chthonic Shamanic praxis. This spirit of the Black Thorn acts as an intermediary between the lesser and greater Saturnian spirits between Nahemah the realm of lunar and sub-lunar spirits and Sathariel the sphere of Qlipothic Saturn one of the unholy trinity within the Qlipoth . After the consecration of Datura I took my scrying mirror and smoked the dried leaves. The results were astounding.

The first manifestations upon my mirror was moth and the bat. As well as the ever shifting beautiful and crone-like aspect of Datura when I called her. Next was visions of tunnels and Draconic eyes that lead me to a great tree. Before this tree were five figures with a stag in-front of them. The figures encroached upon the stag and struck its head clean from its shoulders. I was instructed to go deeper. I went deeper, and looked into the symbols and goddesses across cultures who are associated with the moth, tree, deer and the number five; ultimately, finding the Aztec Goddess Itzpapalotl. Within Itzpapalotl's domain the reader will be interested to know that the Obsidian Butterfly, weather one chooses to identify this as Bat or Moth is her nick name. She is a skeletal, Chthonic goddess who rules over an underworld entitled Tamoanchan - the realm of children who die in child birth and well as women who die delivering them.

She is associated with the moth, Rothschilda Orizaba from the genus Saturniidae according to various internet research. So we have a goddess who is the ruler of a realm of dead children, it is no secret Hebrew lore describes Lilith as the taker of newborns. A goddess of the Cihuateteo (woman who dies during child birth) Just as Ninlil gave birth to the moon god and was banished to the underworld to give birth to yet more Chthonic spirits. As well as according to the Aztecs the Cihuateteo were shades attributed to the west wind which also bears a great resemblance to Lilith. A Goddess corresponding to a moth family with the convenient familus of (Saturn)iidae who can manifest as a beautiful seductive woman or one of terrible might. These Saturnian spirits have a lesser home within Nahemah and a fully manifest home within Sathariel governed by Lucifige Rofacale.

Interestingly enough Itzpopalotl is considered a demon of the Tzitzimime, Star demons who attack the sun during solar eclipse. Legend has it the Tzitzimime fell from the sky with her other demonic conspirators some of which having form of scorpion and toad. To further elaborate on her animalistic manifestations she can also be represented within Aztec culture to a two-headed deer. The Tzitzimime are five in number. Tlaltecuhtli, Coatlicue, Citlalicue, Cihuacoatl, and finally their leader, Itzpapalotl. The author is still meditating on the significance of the five within the scrying vision as reflections of the five accused nations or the five Tzitzimime. More than likely there are a myriad of connections within both.

Blood offering to a Tzitzimime. Codex Tudela, folio 76

Finally, Itzpapalotl and her Tzitzimime, or Lilith and her Lilitu correspond with this poignant image of Tamoanchan. That of a tree split in two with a fountain of blood emerging from the center.

This image should be apparent to those of the black flame to represent the tree of life split asunder, allowing the blood line of the dragon to flow forth. Should one, even with-out Datura choose to focus on this with dedication to the tradition of usurpation and lawless becoming, the gate to the black earth will become apparent. None of these insights would have been gained without the assistance of the spirit of Datura which the author believes to be one of the various servitors of the Great Lilith's spirit.

Now to a more practical application, How can this effect you ? The author wants to give a heartfelt warning to those choosing to use Datura. There is a reason why she is poisonous, there is a reason why she kills and destroys, frequently, wayward teens and the unwary. Yet when one approaches her with the correct veneration and sacrifice within any Satanic current she can hold the keys to the underworld. From the information presented the author suggests making a talisman. Should those worthy, providing proper sacrifice and dedication towards their altars learn the correct ingredients towards their own lawless becoming, this talisman will increase the altar and practitioners power within the first gate of hell manifold. Which in turn leads to stronger manifestations of those spirits within a scrying mirror, dreams, and every day life.

Statue of Coatlicue
National Anthropology Museum
Mexico City

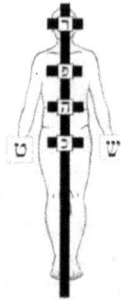

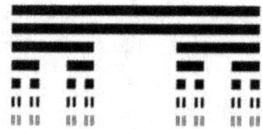

ATTO 719

PT 1: PORNEIA
PT 2: ALOGOS

πορνεία

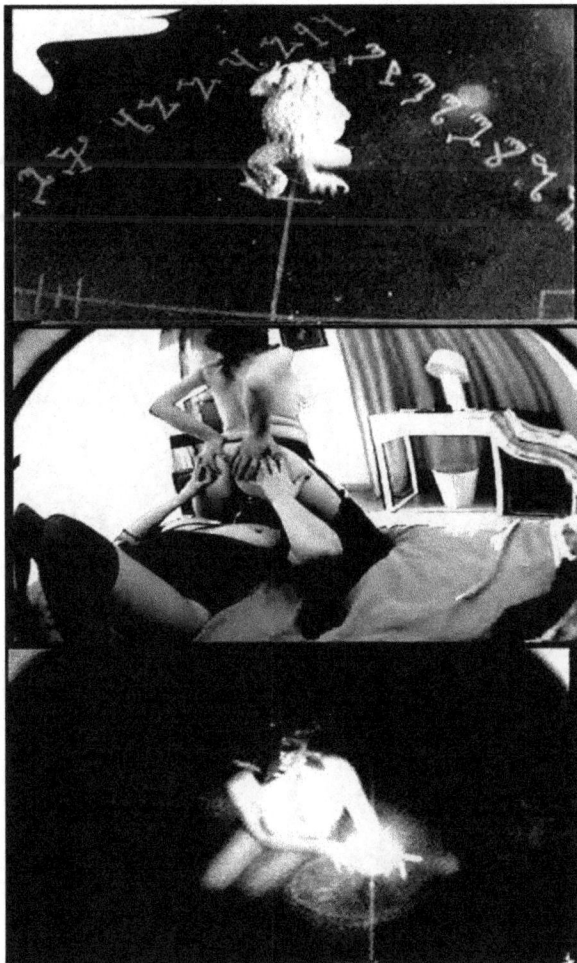

```
We overthrow Hod as an act of abstention
        the cause-effect structure.

  We replace the Passion to the Will
   with the awareness that Holiness
         pervades the matter.
```

ἄλογος

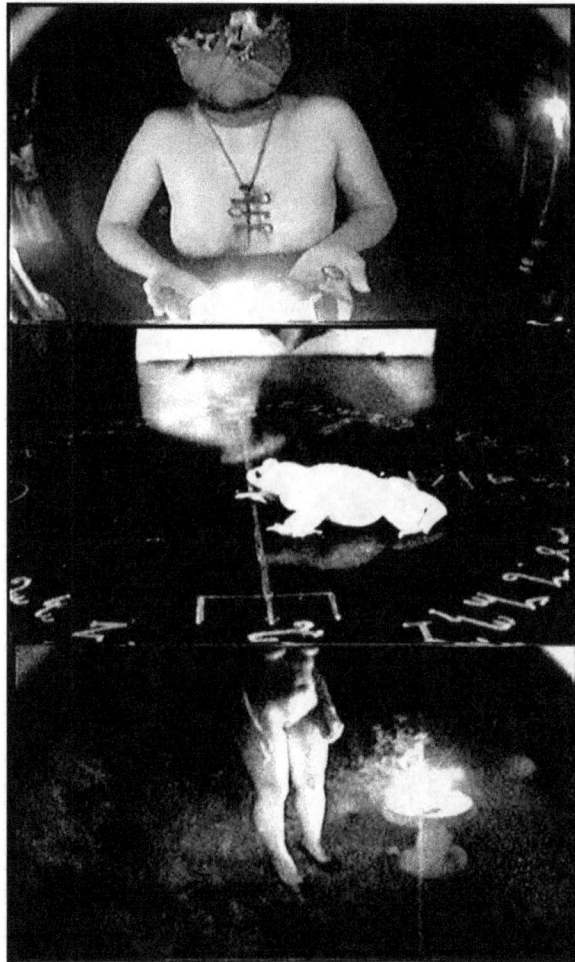

Our action is a centripetal motion against
the Aristotelian non-contradiction theory.

With our work we align ourselves with the
chaotic structure of the Universe.

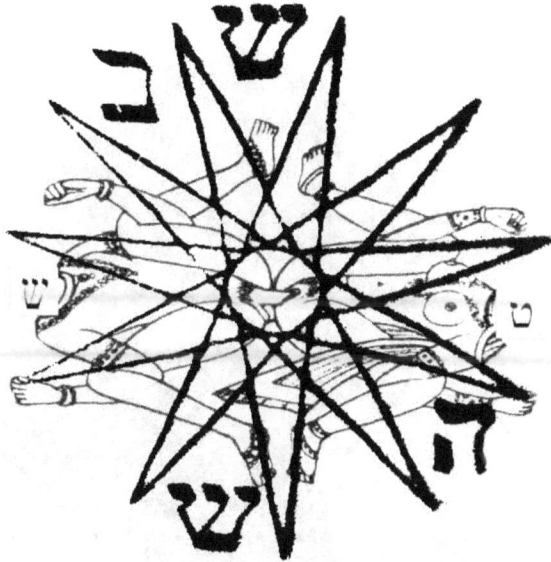

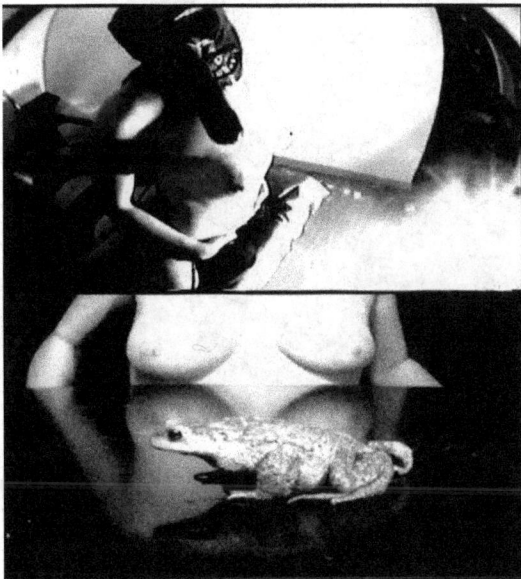

JOIN US !!

KNIFE CODEX: The Cult of Primordial Weapon

Danilo Coppini (L.T.J 49)

Introduction

At the making of man, no natural weapon was given to him. Weak and susceptible to inclement weather, he counted only on his survival instincts to develop weapons, tools, and strategies that helped him to overcome all obstacles. With soft skin and no claws or fangs, he found in nature what was necessary to balance the Predatory Law.

Looking at things from a cold and rational perspective man has always been prey for more aggressive and predatory species. If the purpose of man was to be prey for the other species, then the advent of the knife completely changed the intention of creation and it was a big mark in the history of mankind, a powerful and lethal Goddess of Death and Survival. The knife is the manifestation of the balance that was not granted to man at his formation. It's the physical manifestation of a greater power, an artificial claw created by death itself and presented to men in a crucial moment of their evolution.

In this contemporary universe of paleontology and archeology there are scientific suggestions strong enough to suppose that the ancestors of homo habilis had some ability to use primitive tools to slaughter animals and bone its prey. In certain Kenyan and Ethiopian archaeological sites there were found fossilized bones over three million four hundred thousand years old whose marks indicated the utilizations of rudimentary instruments, ancestors of the first blades, in the activities of hunting and food preparation. Today paleoanthropologists have discovered stone blades manufactured deliberately more than five hundred thousand years ago, shapes impossible to have been made "randomly" by nature. Most likely knives originated with splintered stones, flint, obsidian (a type of volcanic glass,) and meteorites, but they were being improved according to human needs. Throughout the evolution of man, stone blades were replaced by bone, wood, and posteriorly, and then, after the advent of metallurgy, bronze, copper, iron, steel, ceramics, and titanium.

We can't put an exact date on when man first used these tools to attack other men. Most likely, since our ancestors lived as nomads in small groups, they ended up fighting for the defense of occupied territory (where food, water and shelter existed). War instincts such as these are found in other species that live in packs, wolves, ants, and chimpanzees for example. The groups that killed and dominated more effectively grew in numbers and conquered great er territories. The art of killing was the key to survival and all opportunities to destroy rivals should be used. This meant that they were not only required to be masters of offensive attacks but also defense. Ever since the earliest of ages man has developed techniques to attack and preserve his space. It is a fundamental salient that humans are the fruits of war. Only successful warriors were able to mate and "pass their genes forward." Man created armies and all of the primitive concepts of community were based on such alignments. Weapons have transformed man from prey into the greatest predator of all history.

To master the blade was the same as being graced with a sacred gift. The clawed man (in all variants) performed his bloody rituals and gradually these rituals were being rooted as part of war itself. War became an art and weapons the embodiment of divine powers.

The fascination with the blades goes beyond all ages. The knife is the great symbol of survival, hunting, feeding, protection, prosperity, domination, and hierarchy. This instrument became so present and fundamental to the human race that it was absorbed into the religious plots of many diverse cultures. Gods and goddesses everywhere flaunted their blades by subduing enemies and imposing their parameters of Justice and Ordinance, superstitions and legends appeared all over the world, and the rustic survival tool assumed a sacred place.

CHORONZON III

The Formation, Apogee, and Fall of the Gods of War

The great majority of deities were born out of human phobias. At first the gods were built based on 'superior' animals and natural events that the groups could not reproduce. The notion of divinity began to exist as a form of man to materialize everything he did not understand. 'Father and Mother Gods' have sprung up in all cultures to protect their fear-filled 'children' and have been constituted according to the values of each folk. The gods received shapes of raptors (totemic), the strength of felines, and other strong animals (buffaloes, elephants, snakes, and bats, amongst others), the elemental domain (fire, air, earth and water), wings, Skins and / or impenetrable scales, power to contain or promote death, mastery and influence in various thoughts and weapons.

At this very point we realize that many Gods and Goddesses were not created to corroborate humanity but to cripple it for centuries to come. Fear (in the various forms of phobias), caused the gods to sit on the thrones of collective memory where they perpetuated generation after generation as a reflection of the yearnings, desires, and failures of the people who created them. However, as had been previously reported, man had made war a complex and broad art, a creed and a religion. A warrior can be compared to a priest and his weapons, especially the blades, are his connecting points, his sacred icons, his works of art and the receptacle of his own ancestral shadows. Unlike the other gods and goddesses generated from fear and ignorance of nature, the War Gods were built to exalt the "human-predator," the adversities devastator, the bearer of the artificial claw that could fight in equality with all Animals (opponents) previously feared and deified. The Gods of War were projections of what men should be. In analyzing the evolution of some gods of this nature, we find that there are strong traits with (preceding) deities associated with the power of fertility and this corroborates with the concept that only to the greatest warriors were offered the most beautiful women in order to ensure the continuity of blood And a biological formation without fragility. In other cases they were associated with agriculture, which demonstrates the ambiguous nature of weapons and, at the same time, the protection of livelihood (one of the great causes of war).

There were gods who carried 'lightnings', magic sticks, some threw fire from innumerable other fanciful attributes. These gods could not be a reflection of men, after all, they portrayed only what men could not achieve or could not physically / mentally understand, but when a War God was worshiped in his representations, he did not show objects that were beyond reality. These gods carried muscles, armor, and weapons. Regardless of the culture / group to which this god belonged, his powers were within reach of men and were part of the physical life of society. A God of War could be represented by a mythical hero or a historical warrior.

Man have lived in groups since remote times and these social groups have created his own structures. When something goes against this composition, there is a strong pressure to suppress these opposing ideas, and war (conflict / combat) is the way to guarantee and impose superiority. Man justifies his murderous desires and impulses behind innumerable excuses, but we have full conviction that it is an instinctive reaction or even a subconscious action for domain. However, the evolution of society has created lamentable point in our structure by suppressing the ethics of violence and virility, constantly imposing moral values that inhibit combat instincts and promote education to "unlearn" war as well.

The disastrous result was the construction of a tamed society. The Gods of War were being weakened and transmuted according with the exaltation of passivity began to overlap the 'predator-man'. The power - representation of the group organization that guarantees the ordinance of all structure - was gradually being removed from the hands of the warriors and being exercised by men with more diplomatic rather than aggressive inclinations. The consequence of this transition was the emergence of Gods who were molded from a dual essence, after all, war continued to exist, but more veiled and hidden under a mask of Justice. The worship of the ancient deities was falling into oblivion or being adapted as part of a completely enslaving and manipulative plot. This was because warriors began to be restrained from diplomatic decisions. Again, we see gods submissive to the evolution of man.

The powerful genes that were inherited by man were being replaced and old, defeated phobias returned in greater numbers and intensity. Man, like his Gods, became weak, oppressed, blinded spiritually and physically, and tamed by hundreds of codes of conduct. As the incapacitated had the opportunity to exercise power, they created rules to protect them and learned that the art of war should be taught only to the group that would protect this newly created model of society. Kings and Queens became trained dogs in the hands of manipulators in the name of the Law and the population returned to being made up of prey.

CHORONZON III

The Father and Mother of All Weapons

All the transformations that took place in the world were influenced by disputes. Regardless of the 'Culture of Fragility' imposed on men over the centuries, weapons bravely resisted and perpetuated. A small chipped stone was much tougher than societal beliefs and models. The apogee and decline of the great warriors and their gods caused the evolution of weapons to become driven in mysterious ways and adapted to the time and space but still without losing the majesty. The energy of these mortal instruments is still alive, despite the numerous attempts to ban and restrict them.

The knife is the Mighty Father/Mother of All Weapons. We understand that a knife can be understood as follows: Every sharp object that can be wielded can be considered a knife. Thus, swords, sabers, tridents, axes, spears, arrows, maces and even firearms are direct descendants of this primitive tool. Objects built to protect bodies (shields, helmets, and armor) are considered indirect descendants of the same ancestral matrix. Unlike men who have had their strong genes subdued, the "genes" of knives have remained intact for thousands of years, after all, it was not first conceived as only a combat weapon, but also as a necessary tool for the survival of men. Poetically, knives are the expression of balance, of perfect love, of awakening in face of the problems of survival, and their uses are the same from the primitive eras to the present days - which includes disputes, hunts, and murders.

The vast majority of human beings manipulate them daily, mechanically, without imagining all the history hidden in the blades. This ignorance is a natural consequence of the return to the state of 'food' (now measured in energetic levels). The genes of our warrior ancestors were buried under a thick layer of pacifist and egalitarian submission transmitted generation after generation. We are the product of fear and all of our thoughts are slaves of clay molds made throughout hundreds of years. Man believes that he possesses freedom of thought, however, this is a false sensation fueled by invisible barriers contained in our own psychic labyrinths, the fruits of a transgenerational inheritance.

The Soldier and the Warrior

The great majority of men do not know how to differentiate a soldier from a warrior. In fact, historically, there have been incidents where the classifications have merged, that is, a soldier became a warrior or a warrior became a soldier. But under no circumstances can we understand this as a rule.

We define a soldier as a person who works, voluntarily or not, in the armed forces or militarized patrols of a certain sovereign region. They receive a specific and gradual training and, throughout these activities, use military equipment to carry out their functions. They are governed by Major Laws and Internal (Military) Laws that determine their conduct, how they behave and react to certain adversities. The function of a soldier is to dedicate his life (or a determined time of it) to defend militarily the interests of his homeland.

The warrior is classified as a person who fights for his own interests, goals, and dreams with strength and determination. He has great personal abilities that naturally come out in moments of precision. There were peoples in the past who have stimulated such impulses within their members since a young age, such as the Maoris and the Vikings. Warriors usually defend their ideals with vigor and intensity, are belligerent, committed to what they believe to be

41

the right path, and do not position themselves neutrally in situations that have opposite poles. Warriors are committed to their goals because unlike the soldiers, they fight for what they believe to be right and not for what is determined to them. Warrior impulses are contrary to apathetic or phlegmatic impulses. A warrior is not a threat to society, but he does not surrender to everything imposed on him. A warrior has an internal code created from various life experiences that is capable of guiding his decisions. Warriors exalt courage, bravery, loyalty, and honor. Not all have access to weapons and military training, however, they do not avoid combat when necessary. They struggle with everything within their reach.

"Difference between Soldier and Warrior:
The warrior knows which battle to obstinate or give up.
The soldier follows orders."
-Alber Germânio

True warriors do not follow orders blindly and have a questioning tendency. They fight for what they believe in to the point that they will even give their own lives if necessary, always considering their thoughts before every act, after all, they are own their own 'Scales of Justice'. When they make a mistake they have the honor to apologize and repair it if necessary. What makes a warrior brilliant is the ability to join projects that exalt their personal characteristics, motivating them to achieve their goals. By having a war like nature, (both internally and externally when necessary,) everything that helps him to become what he really is becomes necessary at some point along his evolutionary journey.

Warriors are forged in iron and fire, in the heat of personal disputes, and their motivation is what makes their acts so powerful, after all, those who fight for what they believe in are allied with overcoming. This is one of the main foundations of Knife Cult.

Photos: Fig. 1- Danilo Coppini / Fig. 2- Zeis Araujo
Symbol: "The Constant War"
English translation: Nathan Portela
Correction by David Simmons (Hanged Man's Seed)
This text is part of the Knife Codex project.

Atu 18 MOON
Oil on board
Erica Frevel
Private commission by Bölþorn;
an initiate of the Seven-fold Sinister Way

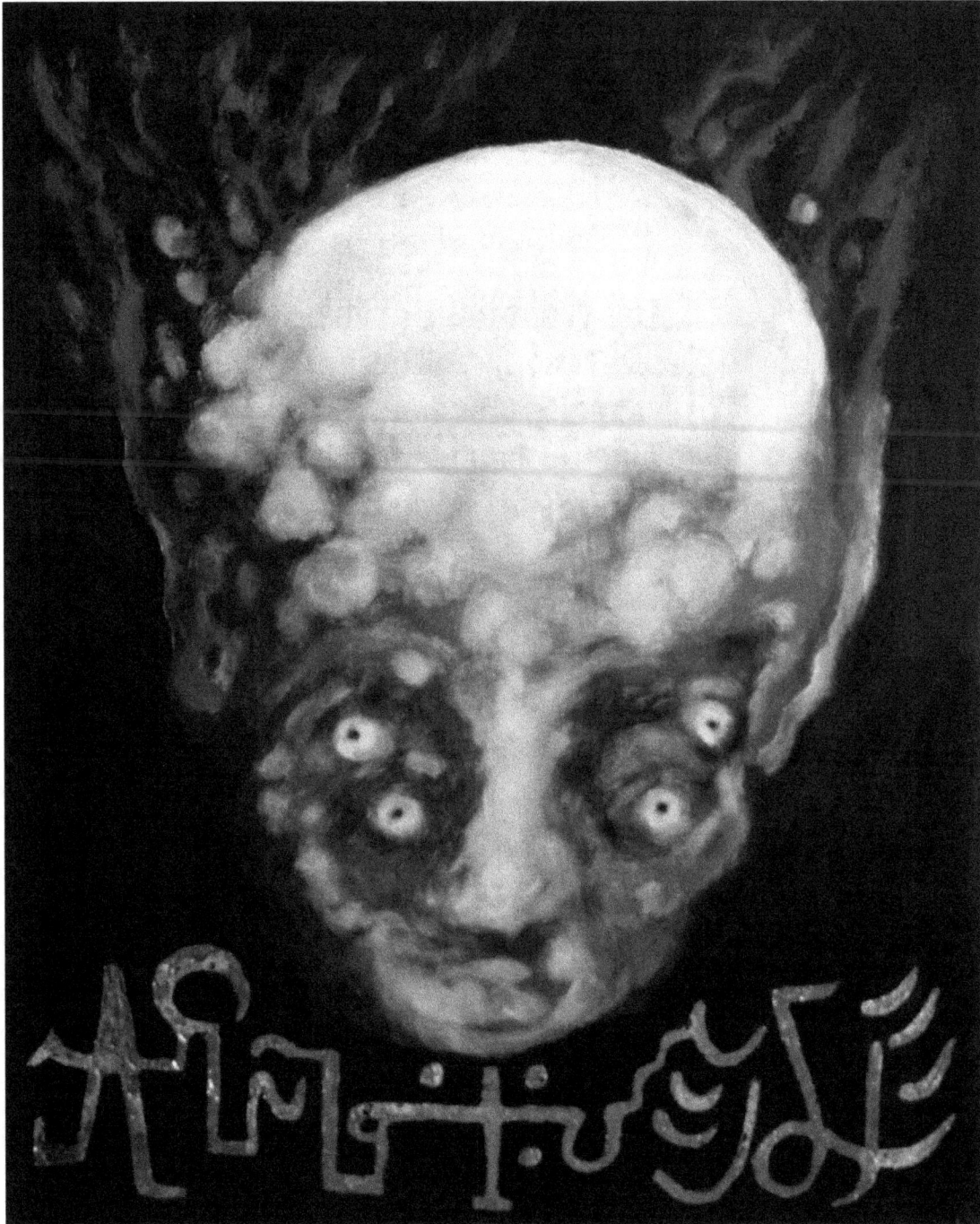

Portrait of Mutating Fire Demon in Astral Form
Oil, blood and goldleaf on board
Erica Frevel
From the private collection of DD Chainsaw

Star Coffin

VAMAPALAH,
TEMPLE OF NIGHT

Rise from your grave,
Deepest mother of dreams.
I twist reality for your return,
And bind the hands of prayer,
With razorwire.

Blood drunk,
On the incandescence,
Of militant dragonism,
From a foot soldier of night.

Come again the ways of strength.
Come with nightmare gaze.
Return from death,
The cackle of laughter's flame.

From this red whetted blade,
The key to your star coffin congeals.
Opening eternity,
From whence the final darkness roars.

Last Fire
Ink and blood on paper
Erica Frevel

The Traveler

On a plain grey platform, I wait for the train, pacing back and forth alongside the other travelers. There is a span of boredom which I fill with thoughts of luggage and small familiar objects that might fill the luggage. A collective movement of heads toward the left of the horizon snaps me out of my thoughts. The train arrives on time and we all nod in agreement that this is our train. This is why we are here. I step back to allow all the other travelers to enter a series of thin doorways into the train. Faces fill the windows and look out onto the platform where they stood only a moment ago. The last of the travelers enter the train but I pause without knowing why. I see the luggage being unloaded from the undercarriage by men who don't speak to each other. A distinct wet slamming of meat against concrete. There are oddly shaped, lumpy, poorly wrapped packages on the platform with me. I stare at them until the train whistles at me, pushing me to make a decision. I lean over the packages and feel the cool shadow of the locomotive move forward on its timely journey. I am alone with the packages. I unfold the outer wrapping of thick black plastic. There are bodies of young girls with no heads. I search for the heads in the mound of packages but cannot find any. The flesh is streaked tan and baby blue. Part of it is dead and part of it is still living. I wonder, whose luggage is this?

A tall man in a thick black pea-coat and leather gloves moves toward me from the far end of the platform. He walks with steady soft steps directly before me and the luggage. He tips his brimmed hat, smiles with exposed teeth and asks if these are my packages? I tell him that they are under my care now, as they are unclaimed, but I am not a thief. Were they his on the train? He tells me he only has use for the heads, that I am free to claim the rest with no ill will from him. I stoop down to unwrap a thick red cord around the black plastic to expose the entire length of a female body. I run the back of my middle finger along the open wound of the throat, between the cold separated breasts, graze the navel and feel the course blond pubic hair in between my fingers. The man nods toward me and indicates that I am to follow him.

"Bring your newly acquired gifts with you."

He walks with measured steps past me and waits for me near a freight elevator. He holds the doors for me with muscular gloves hands. I carefully drag all the bodies into its spacious cage. I arrange them just as they were with the exposed body on top of the others. He smirks at my caution in arranging them. He asks if any of this seems familiar. I tell him no.

"I am just a traveler who missed a train."

He slowly shakes his head in disagreement. His thin mouth hangs open a moment before he speaks again. He has a strange eastern accent I cannot place. He clenches his teeth and moves his tongue oddly at the end of his statements. He speaks another language to himself inside the privacy of his closed mouth.

"You are no longer a horizontal traveler. Trains charge forward only toward the horizon or away from the platform man has built," every word ringing with a metallic tone that I can almost taste in the air. It gives me a sharp pain behind my eyes to listen to him.

He retracts his arm into the elevator and the doors close. There are no buttons to indicate floors. He makes a series of crossing gestures with his index finger in the air between us. The elevator jerks itself free from its inertia and we start to descend. Slowly at first, just like the man's gestures. He steps closer to me. Closer again. He is standing over me and the packages. He is breathing but only barely and I can see his lack of breathe as the elevator becomes colder. I wonder how far we are descending to bring about such change in temperature. I place a hand in my pocket to appear unfazed. The further over me he leans the faster the elevator moves. He searches my face for signs of distress. I do my best to remain straight faced during his inquiry. Without breaking eye contact he raises his left hand and extends his fingers upward. The elevator quickens its pace. We begin to move with such speed that I can feel my consciousness slipping away. I feel the blood rushing away from my face to be replaced with cold numbness. I almost ask him to stop. He finally clenches his fist in the air with the sound of creaking leather and the elevator gently stops. The doors slide open and he politely moves aside and lets me pass by to unload the packages. I line them neatly on the dirt floor before looking up to decide where we are. There are no trains. There are no platforms. I can't tell where we came from because there is no elevator anymore. There is only an undulating darkness where we had just been. It becomes clear that there is no way back.

He claps his hands together three times and separates into two identical men. They both clap their hands and a dozen filthy mutated creatures emerge from the dirt and swing their hips to slap their hideous feet toward the two men. The men point at the packages.

"Bring the lady's gifts into the holding place."

They obey their orders and work together to lift each body before loping over the side of a hill. They disappear in the darkness beyond us. I imagine the blond pubic hair becoming dusty and grey.

Unencumbered by any further loading and unloading, I am free to search the landscape. There is a sky but it has no sun. No moon. There is only a dim greyness emanating from above that sheds so little light that I am forced to move my face very close to what I am inspecting. I trip over something. I pick up a pale blue shoe and lift my left foot over my right knee to determine if they would fit. They are too small. I see another pair of pale yellow shoes with ornate straps. They too are not my size. The men laugh to each other while looking on at my activities.

"Leave what you cannot carry," they say in a metallic harmonized voice.

They each gently put a hand on my shoulder and lead me downhill. There is dust kicked up on our path and cracking sensations underfoot as we move together. It grows colder and colder down the hill and my ears pop from the altitude change. I jerk my head to catch what I think sounds like music from another time wafting through the dead air. I slip and lose my balance and they let me fall forward despite their grip on me. I catch my fall on a thin skull and crack it with my weight. I pick shards of the skull out of my hand and the men seem delighting and surprised by a trickle of blood from my palm.

They glance at each other and then say to me,
"All blood is welcome here."

I see such perfect skulls all around us. Some are stacked together as if they are part of a structure beneath us. I am taken by the sheer amount of bones and skulls, every one unique in shape, the colors ranging from burnt orange to a perfect lily white. The men notice my delight. I ask them if I may take some with me? I have a shrine. I want to use them for my shrine.

One of the men reaches into his pea-coat and hands me a green velvet satchel. I fill it with three skulls after examining them closely like choosing ripe fruit.

"The bodies were gifts. Erotic life. Flesh and hair. Take the skulls to your shrine if you wish."

They hurry down the hill past me. I try to keep up but they are leaping over bones in front of each other. There is a large black car, an older model, waiting for them. One opens the passenger door for the other and enters the driver's side himself. I make my way to the car clutching the satchel so the skulls don't bounce together and crack. I pause like I paused before the train. I can see my reflection in the rear window and I look sick. My eyes are sunken and my skin is pale and turning purple around my mouth. I tell myself it is only the effect of the strange dim light from the sky. I move my hand toward the door and it opens for me. I slide inside the dark vehicle on the rear passenger side. There is only one man in the car. He is the driver.

"You have chosen three of death's heads. They are yours now. But they were not gifts like the girls of flesh and hair. You must give payment before you reach your shrine again."

I am confused about the gifts and the flesh and the hair and the bodies and the skulls. I can't remember accepting any gifts. Who gave them to me? I can't even remember what the destination of my train was. There is no way back to the train platform now and I know this. There is only a path downward. A further descent into the musty cold. Why did I want the skulls so badly? What did I think they could do on my shrine that they hadn't done on the hill of bones? Even so, I thought it ill advised to recant.

"What will you accept for payment?"

The car slows to a stop and the man spins around to meet my gaze. He smiles and I am both terrified and comforted.

"A transformation. I can show you."

He reaches into his pea-coat again and pulls out a revolver from an inner pocket. It is well shined and new. He nods for me to take it from him. I reach my hand out and grasp the top of the barrel. I pull it into my lap with the velvet covered skulls. I carefully push open the cylinder to count the bullets. There are only two.

The other rear door opens and the man's twin enters beside me. Now they are both looking at me and the gun.

"Transform him. He has wronged me."

Before he could finish his sentence I have a vision flash before me. I see the man with two entry wounds in his head. One is on his temple and the other is above it to the right. I see myself opening the door and kicking his body out of the car. He is heavy and I have to kick him twice to push his weight fully away from me.

"Transform him. Give me payment."

I don't understand how he could have wronged himself. Now the man beside me is staring forward at the identical driver. I'm afraid that if I kill one, the other will die. Neither of them show any hesitation.

The driver bellows without anger, "TRANSFORM HIM. THIS IS MY PAYMENT."

I raise the revolver toward the man's head. He doesn't look at me. I feel my finger on the trigger. I feel its slight resistance. I aim at his temple. I squeeze twice and see him slump over as the empty casings ping against the window and roll under the seat. There is a red hole in his temple and another nearby. I reach over to open the door and kick him twice just as in the vision. The weight of his torso pulls the rest of him down. Blood runs off the interior of the door and the dust below swallows it, taking it deep within itself like a parched animal. The door closes itself.

"Your vision is your action. There is no difference now. You have paid one of three debts to me."

I try to hand him his revolver back by the handle but he waves it away. I open the top of the satchel to put it inside. Something is wet. One of the skulls is

51

growing flesh. It smells like rotten meat instead of dust. The satchel turns a dark emerald green with the fluid it is absorbing.

The driver moves the car forward as he answers a questions I never asked.

"This place is not the garden of Eden."

I ask him where the road leads then, if this is not a garden?

"The Citadel."

Portrait of Jayalalita Devi Dasi
Ink on paper
Chapel of Astaroth

Untitled
Ink on paper
Chapel of Astaroth

Andura
Ink and blood on paper
Chapel of Astaroth

Three ov Wands
Ink on paper
Chapel of Astaroth

Pilgrimage
Zoran Antonijevic

We are walking
Silently through the desert
Looking at the skies
Stars are winking at us
Tartish guideposts
Flickering Heavenly neon-lights
For the angelic whorehouses

There's no way we can go
It is so far away
Only a miracle
Can lead us to that eden

It is uncertain
What if at the end of the road
You become me
And I become you
Like back then, when
We were walking the Holy Mountain
Following the coo
Of the pigeon flock
Which led us to a recluse
Where we realized nirvana
While we voiceless fucked

Never mind, let's go
The ride is coming
From the cloud descending
Holy Archangel

You ride him first

S&M Ritual

Zoran Antonijevic

When I hear it
How much you beg me
To love you
When I hear
Tears hitting the ground
I will find mercy for you
Like a god

On your breasts
I will light up briquettes and incense from Jerusalim

Over your mouth I will tie, with rosary
a goatling bone washed in holy water

Instead of a paper, I will use your skin
That what I will inscribe upon you
With a whip and a scalpel
Is a sacred secret
Which you must
Reveal to everyone
Or forget about
666
slaps in the face

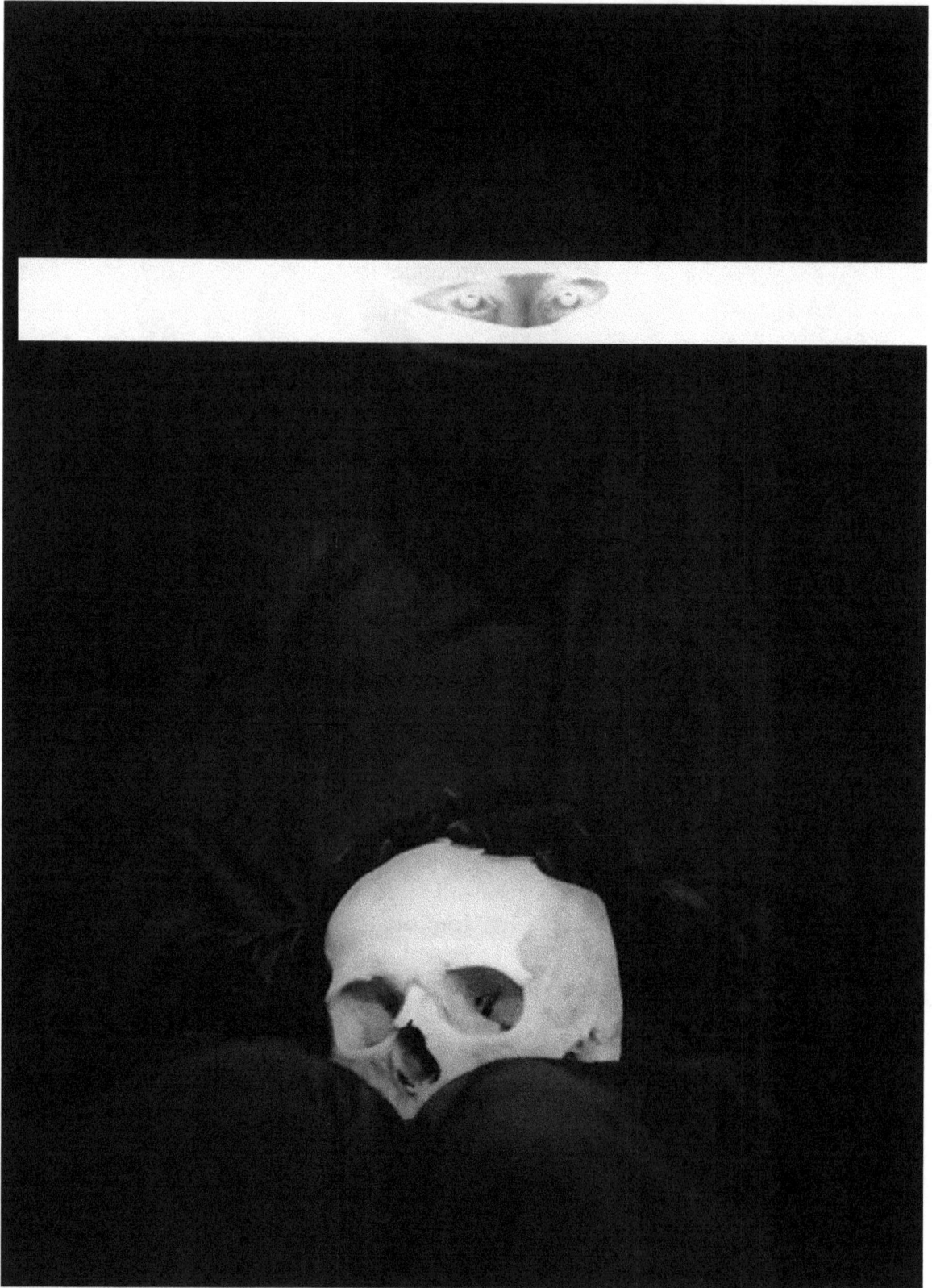

The Devil's Icon

An Interview with
Fosco Culto

The following is an interview with a friend and fellow Satanic artist, Karina Kulyck, better known as her painting pseudonym: Fosco Culto. Born in St Petersburg, Russia, she began painting at a young age before moving to Ukraine where she studied at Lviv Academy of Arts. She has since settled in Livorno, Italy and has representation with Stephan Romano Gallery in NYC. Her paintings can been seen in International occult publications as she is well versed in Black Magic and Satanism. She is also a gifted singer and musician, releasing dark ritual ambient under the pseudonym Lamia Culta. She also works within a musical collaboration known as Corona Barathri. Her demonic paintings are used as album art in her musical projects, effectively bridging her two current disciplines. Despite her notoriously elusive persona, she allowed me to conduct this interview in the summer of 2017.

Erica Frevel: Under what circumstances did you first embrace Satanic worship? Was there an initiation?

Fosco Culto: I consider the year 1999 the date of the transition to the side of Darkness. I saw this Way more noble than following Christian or other religions of light. I was interested in magic, I liked the dark aesthetics. This is the Path of the Singles, and I have always been lonely. There was no information on how to correctly conduct the ritual of self-initiation. But soon I found the right one and spent it in the woods at night. I lit up the first black candles in my life. Then I found two friends with similar interests and we began to conduct rituals in the forest and gather information together.

Erica Frevel: Your paintings hold such intense emotional states. Even the brightest colors invoke a certain darkness and sense of spiritual isolation. Do you experience visions? Are your paintings reactions to your Satanic devotion?

Fosco Culto: My pictures absorbed my emotions and thoughts, because I could not discuss my hobbies and experiences with others. They just did not understand me. I always had to seem simpler. Those who were close, wanted to give me good advice, how to make people like you. I talked on topics that are interesting to them. I was afraid of being alone. I wanted to have company. On the other hand, I so despised people and their idiocy, that directly radiated a negative. People felt it and avoided me. Those who were around had always an excuse to accuse me of my problems and say that I should be grateful to them for the fact that they are still communicating with me. As for satanists - some of them are too far away for real friendship, and some of them I hate and it is impossible to build something useful together. A lot of mad, stupid, perverted and dangerous abusers like the mask of the Devil. Better to stay alone then to stay near such persons.

Now I understand that (after myself) my mother is my best friend and the most reliable person. Of course, I understand that I do not have to listen to everything. But more often than not, she was right. In my family loved art and from childhood I was shown books with reproductions of famous artists. When I began to live alone, I started to paint by oil. At the same time, I investigated satanism and magic. I started with deliberately dark tones, because, like all newcomers, I saw only the invert of white, the wrong side of the light, I wanted to infuriate the people who got into their heads that the flowers and barbie-type are ideal. Therefore, I chose with my favorite music the most vile noise and the most blasphemous bands of the style of black metal, death, grindcore. Black in everything. Black lipstick, black hair, black walls in the house and all just terrible and brutal. This was the stage of Nigredo. Confrontation and Denial of imposed ordinary thinking. In order to appreciate the beauty of the flower and the rainbow - it was necessary to have more experience and thoughts in your head, you had to go through the pain and blackness of the years to fully learn to see the beauty of the entire palette. My mother criticized my first pictures. She spoke, 'there is no space, it's just black colors'. Although now she likes my early works. Then I remembered what the teacher of painting told me when I was 6 years old: black is used in graphics. In painting, black must be excluded altogether. Replace it with a dark color. And he showed examples. He was a kind person and died soon, as many really good people. Many years passed and I completely ruled out the black pigment. Very rarely I use it. I wanted to learn how to transmit Dark without black. The same thing about music - after many years of practice and just

Descent of the Serpent
Oil on canvas
Fosco Culto

𝔥𝔢𝔠𝔞𝔱𝔢 𝔗𝔯𝔦𝔳𝔦𝔞
Oil on canvas
Fosco Culto

life I see Darkness even in the singing of birds. I do not listen to metal. I found a lot of music, in which there is a lot of demonic influence. Blues, for example. Enough dark music. All my life is a Devotion.

Erica Frevel: When I first saw your paintings several years ago they were attributed to a mysterious name: Fosco Culto. Why do you choose to show paintings under this name? Do you think the name will ever change as you progress on your spiritual path?

Fosco Culto: Before I came up with a pseudonym, I tried to sign the first works differently. My name never suited me. When I was 19 I found in the occult book the symbols of evil spirits, and there was an inverted letter "K". There are few works signed in this way. But, I finally decided. I entered the Academy of Art and there I met musicians who invited me to play in a music band. Then I got excited about the idea of playing black metal. And in BM, as you know, all performers use nicknames. One of my favorite bands was the group Darkthrone. From there - "Culto". Now it sounds so funny and prosaic .. But then I was such an impressionable and ideological person, I was also fond of occultism, namely, I was interested in black magic. I knew that I had to build a base for my new personality, to look for a new name. Which will suit me always. My parents divorced and my mother went to Italy. For the Ukrainian people, that meant everything. The Italian language seemed not jaded, like English. Fosco is a word that I liked, it meant "gloomy". Fosco Culto suited me for many reasons. First, it sounded ominous. Secondly, it was impossible to determine exactly who it was - a man or a woman. Because I always knew that the Higher does not have gender, but is a pure energy, essence, phenomenon. Inhuman. Otherworldly.

For a long time I used only this pseudonym, composing music and signing paintings. I refused to perceive my old identity before Initiation. Fosco Culto is the name of the one who creates, this is not a name for everyday life. It gave me strength to go on, to believe in the best. Only once did I want to get rid of this name. There was a hard period in my life. It did not happen unexpectedly. It seemed to me that I had been doing this for a long time, and my world-view was to blame for everything. I was in such a terrible situation that I almost believed that I had been called to come in the flesh of the real Devil, who came to torment me, which destroyed all my achievements and did so that I slowly and painfully died, covered with shame. Before he came into my life, I drew a portrait of the Devil. And a month later I saw this face in reality. The fact is that all the things that I loved, I loved alone. People coldly perceived my achievements. The men I met never considered my talents useful. They wanted children, they wanted a wife, not a person. Although, I think I tried very hard. But some even scoffed at my hobbies. For years we lived like strangers, everyone in their own worlds. And my world was called "idleness," many considered me "cold", "envious," "arrogant." But I was natural. I was Fosco Culto. I explained this to myself - I'm just devoting myself to the Dark Gods, so our roads are so different. And I still believed that I would find my man. And he met me and put me on a pedestal. He listened to my music. He idolized my paintings. He did everything I liked and supported me in everything. And then he threw me down. He showed me that I have nothing to be proud of and I am not worthy of respect, love. He did so that I hated myself. I despised myself. Nobody around loved me. He and everyone around me began to force me to renounce Satan and repent. It meant to deny myself. Kill myself. It was his sick plan. I nearly broke. But, when I passed this test, the glamor was left behind, and the name remained with me. And I still like it.

Erica Frevel: Is it a goal of yours to have your art and music be seen or heard by a mainstream audience or would you prefer it remain underground?

Fosco Culto: I do not think that such art will become mainstream. But I would like my art has seen and heard by many people. That's why I must develop myself and make everything better. Although, at least all things that I do is a proof that I exist.

Erica Frevel: Who are collectors of your work? Are you aware of other occultists using your paintings as altar icons or in their temples?

Fosco Culto: The largest collector to this day is the occult order TOTBL (Temple of The Black Light). Basically, my paintings are bought by people who practice magic and are interested in Satanism. Yes, I heard that reproductions of pictures are readily used as altar images. This always makes me happy. I like very much to decorate my altar and, frankly, many of the works were created for the altar.

Erica Frevel: You create in multiple disciplines; as a singer and musician as well as a painter. If you had infinite resources at your disposal and no one to censor you what would your next creative project be?

Fosco Culto: If no one and nothing could restrain me, I would grow beautiful wings to fly under the Full Moon. Then I would like to become a mermaid with a beautiful silvery tail, swim in a vast ocean to scare people with beautiful songs on the night shores...

CHORONZON III

In the meantime, I am experiencing many limitations that impose on all of us in earthly material existence. I want to continue doing dark music and painting. I would like to start making a video. There are many plans. There are already a lot of work waiting for me this year and next year. Recordings, new paintings, photography, publishing, new friends.

Will
Oil on canvas
Fosco Culto

Nightmare Image of Lilith
Oil on canvas
Fosco Culto

WHITE NIGHT

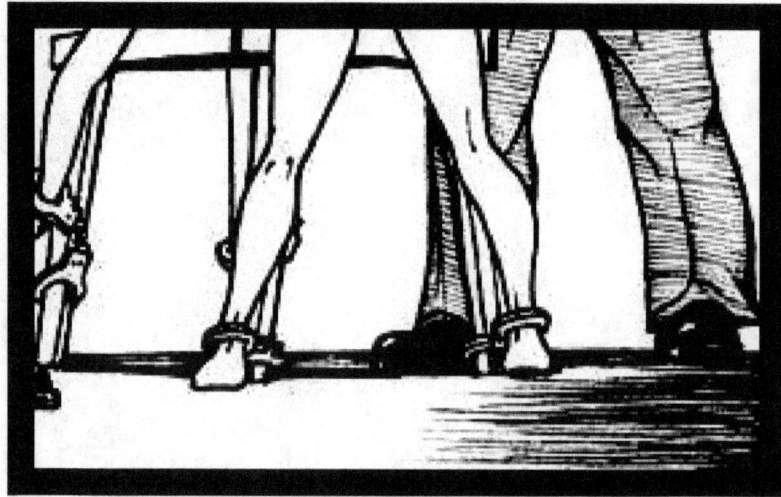

FOR LAUREN

Tempel ov Blood

CHORONZON III

I.

Lauren grabbed her ankles, bending at the waist as clear, crystalline tears began to fall down her face - dropping onto the burnished wood-panelled floor beneath her.

Behind her handler, high-tier within the intricacies of applied intelligence yet also her father, watched and appreciably so as his daughter's skirt began to raise by dint of her positioning - now showing the hint of where thigh met bottom and a flash of panties showing where a burgeoning sex lay beneath.

Incest was the rule here in the secret cult into which Lauren had been born. Those base in their thinking, unimaginative in their ruminations as to what actually constituted the transgressive thought that Lauren's situation and the situation of others like her was mere fantasy.

Far from it.

The deeds that took place on a day in, day out basis amongst so many across the width and breadth of America were exactly like Lauren experienced.

Concerted, concentrated and covert.

Activities that lay beyond the width and breadth of modern, lawful counterparts and pretendus of the "occult" alike - Satanic Ritual Abuse "in the raw."

Lauren's handler teemed with paranoid visions multiple, layered and nuanced according to the severity of the criminal levels which his various acts - both recently performed and those still yet to be enacted - and those latent but soon actionable in conspiracy - would entail should doom befall his activities.

He knew the risks, the potential price to be paid in availing himself of pursuing the very zenith heights of transgressive activity - yet his programming, fluttering on monarch wings, allowed him to press forward - further and further into that which was unknown except to a very minute portion of the populace, and the enactment of which with what amounted to carte blanche only experienced by even a more ultra-elect.

Owen surveyed the area which was before him - his daughter in imminent situation of coming molestation - infrastructure around her which contained so much that was illegal, yet in reality only the rudiment of which were bare necessity for one sworn upon the black for furtherance of "evil without limits" - participation in the same the very base line prerequisite and requirement, the jumping off point from which pleasures unbound awaited the operators possessed of the maximum of will and determination and who possessed the predilections for delectation most discerning, a dispensation of the Dark Mothers themselves.

For Lauren the nail on the floorboard of the home was her point of focus in the position which she now found herself in - dread intermingling with exultation for she like her handler was also seasoned.

In the by and by as her body grew to maturity and with it the agency given to those deemed as "adult" by dint of the law what vistas then would be afforded to her?

Her handler - her blood father - was covert by necessity and, with blood on his hands, some proven yet much more still shrouded within mystery, yet she herself was even more covert for her very youth and station gave her a secrecy nearly unbound in comparison.

She was the hidden rose, the thorns of which were hidden by petals most choice and as such most disorienting - yet none except her handler and those in the program knew the levels of poison which tipped them, nor the razor sharpness which they possessed in their expansive powers to kill, steal and destroy - only latent by dint of her access.

Red levels of alarm were now hers to experience in training as she felt her skirt being raised slowly and then the hand - calloused and strong - grasping and feeling with a tactile sensitivity that its appearance did not belay the contours of her posterior, a finger slipping gently between the hem of her underthings and haunches to flitter ever so briefly upon her sex, still incipient in appearance - long activated in effect.

White Nights were hers to command for as the monarch slave she was in fact the monarch to a degree which others were not - all eyes, never sleeping, upon her - the focal point fleshly for their own program involvement.

She the ever-present vampiric element which supped upon the bodies of the hands that fed her, punished her and cultivated her further and further towards ever-careening levels of consciousness development most arcane - the facilitator of a future earthly dominance most palpable.

The cries of tens of thousands of children like unto her - but none in truth her equal - passed in complex routes unknown and unregistered along the pathways of the grid - the building blocks and mortar, the foundation for her base of terror. She bit her lip lightly in contemplation of the same, one eye cocked jauntily and still focused upon the strange tilt of that one nail upon the floor which was unlike any other as she felt the hands of her handler pull her panties down incrementally, inch by inch, allowing them to rest finally at mid-thigh - air of confined space once dead and lifeless now alive, electric and swirling in direct reaction to her state of now exposure.

Time slowed and then seemed to almost stop altogether as the pressure built - whether an insertion of a choice portion of her handler's biological vehicle, erect and ever ready in such circumstances, or that of a foreign object unknown to her.

Lauren closed her eyes then, allowing the visions of worlds crashing into each other to subside and the interlinking of neural pathways to inaugurate, thoughts compressing upon thoughts - scenes viewed covertly in isolation igniting a prairie fire first to burn throughout her constitution, blaze of the refiner refining, thus primed to burn all that which lay without.

II.

"Open your mouth and lift your tongue, there, that's it..."

Lauren was no longer with Owen but instead with one of the kindly females who frequented the house on an intermittent basis - kindly in outward constitution at the very least, though her agendas as the case may be were without question entirely more foul than her demeanour belied.

Cherubic lips parted in obedience, ruby red in hue without any cosmetic application but purely by the dint of youth and the near incessant sacrifices of mental and physical attention that was poured upon her both by her handler, clientele and fellow-travellers - the latter two demographics more often than not intersecting frequently, the proportion rising as the former became increasingly compromised and found their lives exceedingly under the sway of her father and his associates.

A small drop, then another, then another fell from the mechanism the female adult had removed from the small amber bottle - doses miniscule but felt as they fell upon their fleshly target and as the absorption began sublingually. The lady reinserted the mechanism into the vial, sealing it, and patted Lauren on the head - signalling that Lauren had done her due diligence at least in the inaugural stage. Her small lips closed then, feeling the strange liquid beneath her tongue with its strange absorption, swishing slightly and then swallowing.

Large black banners hung from floor to ceiling, several in number, in the steel building into which she was now led - the fields of black marked three-quarters the way up their expanse with a round circle within which was a thick black swastika. Lauren smiled to herself sardonically, knowing that these specifically were the insignia of a whore - or rather one enslaved to a whore, martyred for a whore by her own insidious and fell manipulations - her monstrous appetite for seduction having moved beyond single men here and there but latterly aimed at the seducing of an entire people. Her swine, weaponized and deployed and ultimately controlled by her own cunt - the hidden and alien mastermind concealed through the rigid, wiry brown-clad suicide troop who was its cut-out in the classical espionage sense of the term.

In the corners others went about their work quietly, self-contained person to person in quiet concentration - the night yet still young, the moving concourse of time marked on the large digital clock near the most central area well-proportioned and indicating to each and every one the time that had been spent and the time yet left. All hurried to reach completion on their individual projects and targets by the moment the red shining numerals reached a certain point, lusting for yet sublimating for the time being their desire to be about other pursuits, latterly.

Lauren had received her ministration openly, overtly in the presence of the others as she always did, for she herself was always primed on these special evenings there among the hive and there was never any question to that fact. The dosing of the others among the retinue of her handler was more deceptive and with more room for apparently random medication - small disposable paper cups of water passed out to each and all at a certain hour, some laced - some not - those drinking not knowing but more often than not hoping that they too would be in the position of being attuned to Lauren in the way that most of them at least once or twice had been accustomed. While randomized and hit or miss in the knowledge of the postulants, Lauren knew that the handler knew - as she often did - who would receive and who would not in most cases than not during those occasions - intentful elements laid down with the crisp precision and brutality of well-seasoned black leather upon naked and supple flesh.

Monitors showed visions pre-determined by the high-tier of their number, chosen carefully and with much deliberation, as speakers liberally arrayed throughout the interior infrastructure broadcast sounds, messages and command prompts sometimes directly correlated with the screen display - sometimes asymmetric to them. The purpose was always the same, however, to induce dissonance and confusion - to bifurcate then trisect the consciousness allowing the dominant consciousness of she, harridan prime, to insert, intrude - to take hold of and in so doing, control. She the center, they the links in the chain of terror.

Lauren sat down upon a divan, dilapidated due to its age and qualitative degeneration yet on these nights altogether regal in its purpose and by dint of the one who it bore. She watched idly as the lady who had administered her dose went about the room, impugning upon the others during the course of their activities - some receiving the active, salient ingredient which would accelerate their participation in the night's coming activities - others imbibing only a placebo.

Her mind wandered as she waited for the narcotic to take its effect upon her consciousness, looking comparatively at the various congregants who possessed biological vehicles feminine in nature and presentation.

Was her own mother among them, knowing that she, Lauren, was her spawn in part - was one of them an unknowing surrogate?

She silently cursed at both possibilities for she rejected the entire concept of conventional motherhood even if enacted under subversive auspices - even then it was too compromising, too sound in nature to allow the furtherance of far-reaching agendas entirely unsound to their every last filament.

She imagined for her own amusement the possibility of one of the women in attendance being possessed of the seeds of life within them even now - on this night - and she relished the vision of herself prowling among them, selecting the lone offender or offenders in the plural and ripping the stillborn fetuses from their very flesh.

She was hostility embodied in the body of not a woman but a girl - already long blooded by the tearing of the shroud of skin which for some indicating the crossing of a formidable threshold into a country entirely new, but still yet not secreting that blood unbidden and internal that marked the possibility for producing another human life. Hers was girlhood, her black power and her very living a vector for anti-life.

III.

She felt her skin became papery to the touch and visions of billions of stars exploding flashed before her eyes which were open, unwavering and dilated to capacity. The bodies of those around her shimmered with strange disturbance, pulsating, and despite their loyalty or perhaps because of it she imagined herself slaying them at the speed of mind, snapping bones and piercing through their flesh and tissue with her hands alone - exploring eagerly their still-living flesh to extract bloodied organs - the once esoteric now exoteric - to hold aloft in grim triumph amongst their garbled screams.

Her handler - father - knew these thoughts and as such she found herself held down, shackled - platinum-toned steel cuffs with correctional black box for further restraint upon her child-like wrists - leg irons upon her ankles, heavy and painful in their bondage. Her clothing, already somewhat revealing, sheared from her body with the type of instrument utilized in surgery.

Now naked, bare and chain-laden in the assembly beneath the sodium lights - murderess in potentia - daughter of Mars, forced devotee of Saturn in communion under duress.

"Suffer the little children to come unto him, for of such is the kingdom of hell. All praise be unto Satan, for he is master of all. All condemnation be unto God, for he is master of nothing."

- Child Killer Rite, The Book of Dark Mothers

Longpig
Collage on board
Erica Frevel

𝕬𝖇𝖔𝖒𝖎𝖓𝖆𝖙𝖗𝖎𝖝

Oil on canvas
Paul Barton

𝔒𝔠𝔲𝔩𝔞𝔯𝔦𝔰 𝔗𝔢𝔯𝔯𝔦𝔟𝔲𝔰

Oil on canvas
Paul Barton

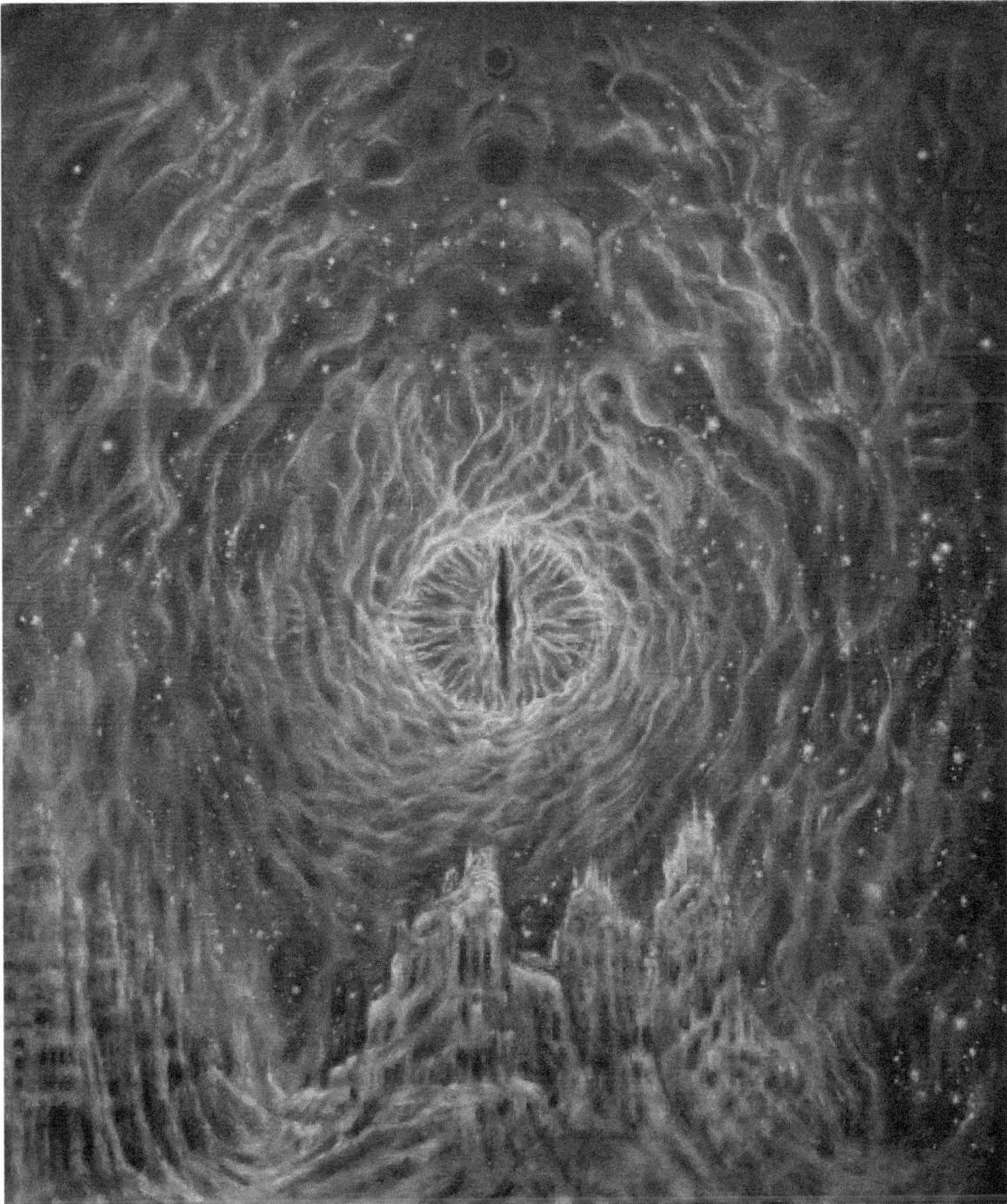

His True Face

Christopher Ropes

Vision 1

It began in fire
And blood,
An inferno laying
A blazing blessing
On the head of
Every man, woman, child,
And gouts of crimson
Spilling down from the sky
And up from
The dark places
Of the earth,
As if every god's throat
Was cut all at once.
The screams of the dying were
An orchestra of the damned and doomed.

I,
Even I,
Was burned and bloodied.
I was stained
And my mouth filled
With the salt and copper
Mystery of death.

When the flames burned low
At last,
And the rivers of blood
Trickled to burbling puddles,
The earth was blackened,
Reddened,
Fat from its corpse feast,
And uninhabitable.

CHORONZON III

Those few of us left
Knew we were not
Long for the world.
Why we had been spared
Was irrelevant.
We were going to die
By the hand of another,
Or our own,
Or else we would waste away
With starvation
Or from whatever new plagues
Traveled on the coattails
Of the apocalypse.

We avoided each other,
Seeking some Satanic enlightenment
And a scrawny safety
In solitude.
We were like the desert fathers
And o, we were tempted.

For days,
Surrounded by visions of copulating demons,
I let my own blood flow and
I prayed over
Three unmarked graves,
Side-by-side,
To my Father Satan,
Knowing not why
This place
Or these three graves.
My prayers were prayers of thanksgiving and joy,
Gratitude for being shown
The coming of
His Kingdom.

On the sixth day,
The dirt of the graves
Began to stir,
To push out and back

CHORONZON III

As the blood-saturated earth
Gave birth
To three living corpses. |

The first,
On the left,
Crawled out of the grave
And slumped
Facedown
At my feet,
But it trembled,
As if vibrations deep
Underground
Shook it,
Ever so slightly.

The second,
To my right,
Stood with a hand
Stretched
To the sky,
Where I saw
The stars were maggots,
Wriggling in distant
Cosmic rot.
The eyes of this
Second one
Were uplifted
And I could not see them,
But its entire attitude
Was of a saint
In ecstasy.

The third stood
Directly before me,
Its eyes locked
Onto mine.
I could barely meet
Those eyes,
Though I forced myself to,

CHORONZON III

Thinking it would not do
To avert my eyes
From the Lord's gaze.
The eyes,
| The eyes
Were full of stars
And the stars
Were the worms of death
And the works of death.
This being
Held out its hands,
Cupping in them
Its own heart,
Seething with living barbed wire,
And it offered this
To me.

In devotion,
Recognizing in these three corpses
My beloved Master,
I took the proffered organ.

The barbed wire tentacles
Wrapped around my hands
And lashed forth
To grip my face,
Barbs digging and hooked
Into the backs of my hands
And my weathered, leathery cheeks
And around my neck.
It pulled itself
Up to my mouth
Whereupon I bit into it.

Black, thick blood
Gushed forth
Into my mouth
And forced itself
Down my throat
With violent life,

84

CHORONZON III

Holy life.
The flesh of the heart
Tore loose
Between my teeth,
Wrapped itself around my tongue
Like a lover's kiss,
And slithered down into my belly.

"Sanctus, Sanctus, Sanctus,"
I chanted.
"I have eaten of your body
And drank of your blood,
But I do not ask
To be saved.
Instead,
Let the song of my torments
Reach the throne of falsehood
And slay the lamb,
Brutalize the shepherd,
Scatter the flock
To the wolves
That devour.

The central figure spoke,
If such could be called speech,
In a voice that was
Sheets of parchment
Brushing against each other.

"You are our true son,
And with all our sons and daughters,
You shall know
The mercilessness of Hell.
Your body will be flayed
Down to the bones
And the bones
Will be sharpened as weapons
To be wielded by demons
Against the throne of falsehood.
To slay the lamb,

CHORONZON III

Brutalize the shepherd,
Scatter the flock
To the wolves
That devour...

"But your soul
Shall be a jewel
In Satan's iron crown,
You shall see
His Kingdom
From atop His head,
Gazing through
His all-piercing eyes.
You can have all this,
To protect your
Insignificant existence
From looking upon
His true face,
Which not even a man's
Immortal soul
May do
And yet live.
Do you accept the bargain?"

And then I wept.
"Have I not been faithful,
That I may not see
His true face?"

The entity said,
"I offer you glory
And salvation."

"Glory and salvation
Be damned,"
I cried.

CHORONZON III

"The prizes of a weak soul.
All I have done
Has been to serve
In the hopes of seeing
His true face.
Your true face."

The corpse nodded
And the starworms in his eyes spun
In ever increasing agitation.
"You have chosen well
And you are worthy,
O Prophet.
Behold our face,
And I shall even grant you
A life on the other side
Of death's maw
That you may tell
Of the beauty and anguish
Of serving Satan."

And then I saw
A Blackness wash over
Blackness,
An ink moving between
The worming stars,
And the ink swallowed
The stars
And their larval souls.
And there were infinite eyes
In that Blackness,
Eyes that I could not see
But looked upon me
With malice and bliss.
The pictures I normally saw
In my head,
The words that normally
Narrated my life,
Were replaced

CHORONZON III

With slashes from an infinity of razors,
The cuts slicing open
My mind and my soul.
All manner of Diabolism
Seduced me,
Murder and blasphemy,
But I was paralyzed
In the rapture.
And the life left my body
Through countless cuts
And the disintegration of my spirit
Under Satan's unveiled gaze.

But life,
As promised,
Was returned to me.
When I opened my eyes,
I was before my altar,
The candles burning low,
And these words in my book.

The vision slipped
Into the wilderness
Of my thoughts,
Where it remains hidden,
Flirting from tree to tree,
Like a hungry ghost
Stalking His prey.

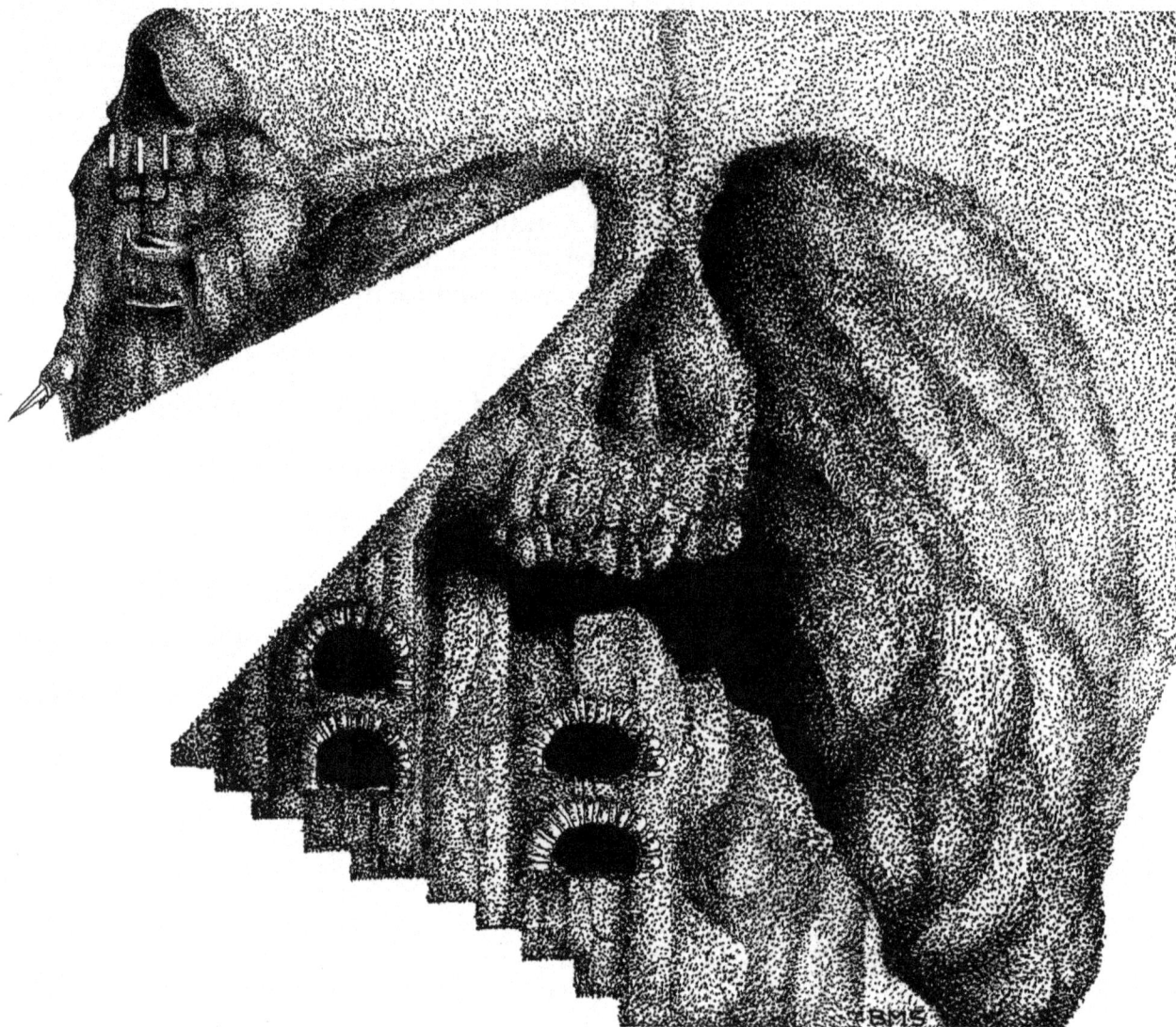

Abyssus Abyssum Habitatis: Meditant

Ink on paper
Bryan Maita

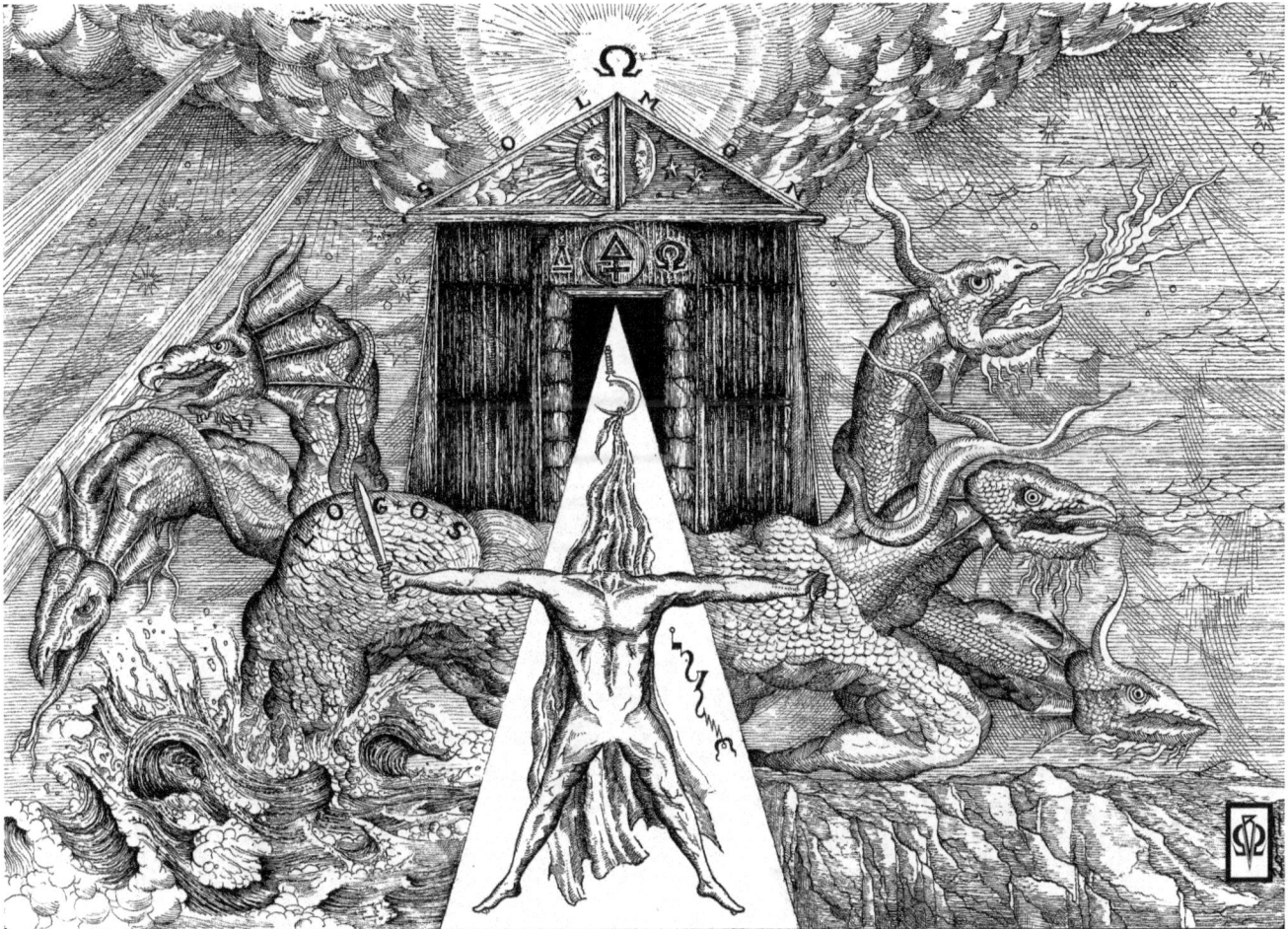

Hermetic Initiation Through
The House of Logos

Ink on paper
Bryan Maita

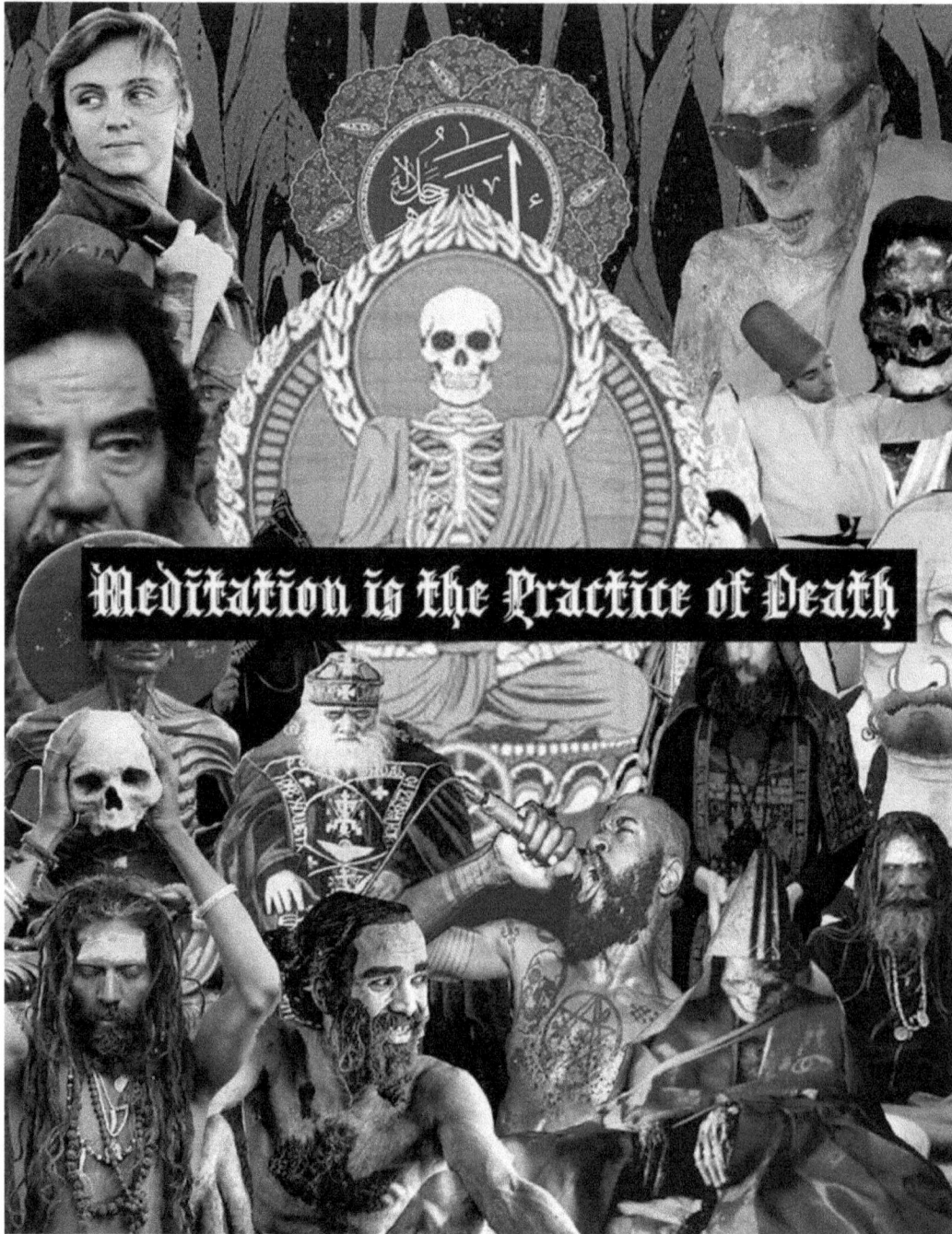

Meditation is the Practice of Death
Digital collage
Nurgul Jones

Psychic Warfare
Digital collage
Nurgul Jones

The Wolf
Black Magick, Cannibalism and Lycanthropy

Erica Frevel

The history and practice of lycanthropy has long been associated with witchcraft and vampirism (blood-drinking aside) due to their common source of power flowing from the Devil. Through Black Magick ritual, there are those who seek to discover a full realization of the sadist within themselves through a relationship with Satan. From the isolated heights of the Carpathian Mountains to the dense jungles of the Valley of Mexico, werewolves have found their hunting ground on the forested perimeter of civilization where night creatures roam freely with the spirits of Evil. Nocturnal sorcery is the feral ritual embodying this evil in the abandoned sanctuary of Satan's sacred ground. The forbidden cult of the wolf is where man finds secret connection to his demon nature; a bloody liberation.

BLACK MAGICK and ASTRAL PROJECTION

It is thought that only through Satanic Magick or the blackest of Witchcraft that a man can master the transformation of lycanthropy. It is the Devil that allows the minds of man to perceive of themselves as predators or demons in the flesh. Whether it is a subjective illusion or an objective physical transformation cannot be determined but the outcome remains the same: a witch befouls the mundane creed to become one of Satan's beasts. Sexual transgressions lead to orgiastic frenzy. The use of hallucinogens (especially herbs of Saturn) are said to aid in the witch's ability to astrally mutate the subtle body. This is one aspect of the mastery of astral projection. Once deep trance has been attained, usually by frenzied dance, it is not difficult to will the "projection of the double" to appear as though a wolf. The common account of werewolves being subject to the pull of the full moon is also indicative of the hormonal, passionate, sexual aspect of the wolf. It is during a full moon that all underlaying emotions come roaring out in humans and animals alike. It can be seen how easily shamanic animal totemism can be combined with the act of feral Satanic magick.

CHORONZON III

Looking to nature for a terrifying sublime connection to Satan, in the vein of Romanticism of the 18th century, we can see how the ravenousness of the wolf makes it the obvious choice for a totem animal. Ripping apart large and small prey alike, the predator utilizes instinct, not law. Within nature we find that only the strong survive in the face of overwhelming indifference. In some ways, this indifference is perceived as demonic by humans. The predator is also a false prophet; a wolf in sheep's clothing who deceives mankind. The wolf's nature is cunning, cruel, savage, treacherous and thieving- they are deceptive outlaws and apex predators who hunts by the dark of night. However, the wolf will also feed upon carrion which further indicates a correlation with Saturn and the greater Saturnine sphere of dark influence.

THE ANTI CHRIST

Wolves were once the most dangerous predators within man's immediate environment. Given free reign to exist in their natural state, they are just as likely to devour a small child as a chicken. This state of remorselessness is anathema of Judeo-Chrisitan morality and the civilizations that uphold it. Anything that violates this morality is therefore demonic in nature, not to mention the deeper cannibalistic aspects of lycanthropy. One can attempt to pray for the divine love of christ's miracles or accept the animal fury within himself.

By choosing to emulate the characteristic blood-lust of the predator, one is also choosing the avatar of the enemy of the lamb of Christ. One is reminded of the hedonistic crimes of Gilles de Rais and Erezebet Bathory in the Middle Ages. More recently, we have the 20th century crimes of the child murderers Ian Brady, Albert Fish and Andrei Chikatilo. All were explorers of the outermost regions of sadism who continually violated laws, both secular and ecclesiastical. For the mourning, frightened parents who lost their young children to the hands of predators, these men are but werewolves - monsters who experience debaucherous pleasure while participating in the ritual slaughter of the innocent. These killers, although from the view of the church are deplorable, are the temporary embodiment of the Antichrist. The wolf's favorite meal is a plump, distracted lamb, meek in its disposition.

WOLF CULT

Across cultures there are strong associations between wolves and what I refer to as the dark gods and their various cults. In North America, there is the Navajo belief in the Yee Naaldlooshii or skinwalkers; witches who practice cannibalism, shapeshifting and necrophilia. At the peak of their black magick teachings they are required to perform a human sacrifice (it is arguable that this is a contemporary practice). The victim is often a family member, which is reflected again in common European accounts of lycanthropy. In Mesoamerica, the Aztecs used the word Nagual to describe humans who could transformed into animals, especially individuals born on "the dog day" of their calendar. Tezcatlipoca, invisible god of divination, chaos and disruption, is known to be the patron overseer of the Naguals. In Greek mythology, Hades is never without his hellhound, the three headed Cerberus. Charon wears a wolf pelt or wolf ears in some descriptions.

Although it may recede into the forest for periods of time, the presence of the wolf cult has circled the edges of human spirituality indefinitely. The völkisch movement in Germany eventually lead to the anthropomorphizing of the Nazi forces as wolfen. There was a pervasive fear of Nazi werewolves, hardcore clandestine operatives employing sabotage, assassinations and ambushes behind enemy lines. Furthermore, Hitler referred to himself "a wolf", named his headquarters "Wolfsschanze" and hired his chief secretary, Johanna Wolf, for love of her surname. The nationwide worship of Hitler as a spiritual figure constitutes a 20th century wolf cult. We continue to see how persistent this cult has been into present times. In the midst of Greek financial and political crisis, there is a resurgence in its native pagan practice, which is now legally acknowledged as a religion. Many young people are turning away from the orthodox church toward their ancestral rituals while more evidence of a wolf cult surfaces. As recently as the summer of 2016, archaeologists digging on Mount Lykaia in Greece uncovered the 3000 year old skeletal remains of a teenage boy under an ash altar. These findings have initially been considered evidence of human offerings to Zeus-Lycaeus, a king who is transformed into a wolf by Zeus in punishment for serving the god human flesh. Zeus-Lycaeus was later worshiped and secretly sacrificed to as a god (hence the prefix Zeus). It is said that the god requires human meat every 9 years culminating in human sacrifice. The sacred mountain site at which these sacrifices took place predates the existence of Zeus by thousands of years.

The area of Upper Egypt was home to the area known as "Lycopolus" meaning "city of the wolves" in the Greco-Roman era. This Egyptian city (now the modern city of Asyut) had a patron deity of war and the dead personified as Wepwawet or Upuaut, who was half man and half wolf. Although there are less ruins in Lycopolus than in other areas, there are bones of wolves in the tombs alongside mummies. This sacrifice of wolves (most likely African golden wolves as opposed to common jackels) is unique to the tombs of Upper Egypt.

The regions west of the Black Sea saw the rise of the Dacians, who are ancestors of ancient Romans, and said to have considered themselves "wolfmen". These Balkan peoples held onto their ancient Neolithic wolf cult from the mountain regions. They were a warrior people whose military initiations utilized hallucinogens and wolf rituals as a means of transforming a soldier into a fearless, bloodthirsty beast. The territory of the Dacians was known widely as "wolf country". The symbol of the wolf is later assimilated with that of the serpent/dragon to make the infamous Dacian Draco used to terrify the enemy in battle. It was in 1436 that the dragon and the wolf became permanently bonded in history as Vladislaus Dracul ascended the throne to defend his ancestral "wolf country" against invading Turkish forces. Bloodthirsty enough to be feared by his own people and enemies alike, Vlad Dracula had a heart that knew no fear or remorse. His decisions were quick merciless, such is the instinct of an experienced predator. The prince was known to kill both mother and child in the most inventively sadistic of methods. Not many could bring themselves to make eye contact with the Voivod; his gaze was thought to have evil, hypnotic powers much like that of the wolf. His torturous yet effective reign of Wallachia led to his current legendary status as the original Vampyr.

Vlad the Impaler
Oil and blood on canvas
Erica Frevel

WOLF RITUAL

There are many recipes for hallucinogenic salves, nicknamed witch's ointment or lycanthropic unguent. They are ritually prepared with the intent to aid in the willful manipulation of the astral body. The most common ingredients are, as stated earlier, the herbs and plants associated with Saturn or the Underworld. Most herbs and flowers listed here grow in cracks or gaps, therefore rooted in darkness. Many names for the herbs used in witch's ointment from antiquity are colloquial terms, sometimes referred to as their "wiccan names'. It should be noted that some modern interpretations for these recipes state many ingredients as common parsley. However, the parsley/celery/carrot family (Apiaceae) itself is not entirely poisonous; it is within the genus Oxypolis and Cicuta that we find the more deadly plants. There is also a notion that one is to harvest these plants in the wild during the corresponding planetary day. If that is not possible, as some are now endangered species (and it is becoming increasingly difficult to obtain the fat of children) there are several alternatives. One can plan ahead and grow some of these plants in a private garden or purchase them and consecrate the plants on the altar individually corresponding to their sacred day.

These salves put your body and spirit in the proper position to achieve astral mutation into a wolf. However, it is the genuine communication with Satan and the utterance of certain incantations that allow the demonic transformative energy to pass between Satan and the witch. In the case of a feral werewolf transformation, one is required to perform a more feral than ceremonial ritual. Rolling in dirt, screaming, biting, ripping one's restrictive clothing off, unrestrained destruction, running wildly and diving into dark pools of water during a full moon are all ways to cast off the human form (astrally as well) in order to run and devour alongside the night-creatures under Satan's midnight cloak. It is the willing spiritual frenzy that is most important in this wolf ritual.

The classic recipes for ointments come from the oldest available source on European witchcraft, namely Johannes Hartlieb's 1456 "Book of all Forbidden Arts: Das puch aller verpoten kunst, ungelaubens und der zaubrey". I have added the scientific classifications for the plants alongside their common names to avoid confusion.

The three recipes are as follows:

Ointment A

- Fat of young children (boiled in a bronze vessel until thick)
- Eleoselinum*   • Celery leaves
- Hemlock   • Conium maculatum
- Aconite   • Wolf's bane
- Poplar leaves   • Soot

Ointment B

- Sium   • Cowbane
- Sweet Flag   • Acorus calamus (mild hallucinogen)
- Pentaphyllon   • Cinquefoil
- Nightshade   • Atropa belladonna
- Choice of oil   • Bat's blood

Ointment C

- Fat of children who have been dug from the grave directly
- Wheat paste to thicken
- Henbane   • Hyoscyamus niger (psychoactive, very toxic)
- Aconite   • Wold's bane
- Pentaphyllon   • Cinquefoil

*Eleoselinum is an old term for celery. At first glance one may not see the significance of including a salad in with your hallucinogens but keep in mind that celery was a Cthonic plant in Greek mystery cults. Its Latin name gives us a hint of the graveyard (Apium graveolens). Its leaves were used to make garlands for the deceased. The plant was said to have sprung from the blood of Kadmilos, father of the Kabeiroi.

CHORONZON III

FEATURED ARTISTS
Portfolio and Contact Information

FOSCO CULTO : Satanic Oil Painter
Livorno, Italy

    society6.com/fosco_culto
    redbubble.com/people/fosco-culto
    artfinder.com/fosco-culto
    foscoculto@gmail.com

VLADIMIR VACOVSKY : Ritual Collage Worship
Prague, Czech Republic

    facebook.com/vacovskyvladimir
    instagram.com/vladimirvacovsky
    vladimir.vacovsky@seznam.cz

BRYAN MAITA : Hermetic Illustrator and Automatic Drawings
Venezuela

    facebook.com/BMS-Illustration-112594042791814
    bjmaita213@gmail.com

BARRY JAMES LENT : Contemporary American Surreal and Esoteric Artist
Westchester, New York (USA)

    barryjameslent.com
    barrylentdevilsdesign.com
    barry10566@yahoo.com

CHORONZON III

NURGUL JONES: Digital Collage Artist
Whereabouts unknown

    facebook.com/DivisionTransgresif

ERICA FREVEL : Satanic Artist
Philadelphia, Pennsylvania (USA)

    society6/ericafrevel
    ericafrevel.bigcartel.com
    instagram.com/negativeaura
    ericafrevel@gmail.com

PAUL BARTON : Occult Painter
Wastelands of Eastern Pennsylvania (USA)

    eldritchvoid.com
    instagram.com/pbarton131
    jcurwen777@gmail.com

KONSTANTYN KOPACZ // WARHEAD ART : Medieval Style Graphic Artist
Lviv, Ukraine

    facebook.com/warheadart
    warheadart@gmail.com

CHAPEL OF ASTAROTH : Devotional ink paintings from the Chapel
Pacific Northwest (USA)
Sao Paolo (Brasil)

    facebook.com/chapelofastraroth88
    instagram.com/chapelofastaroth

V.L.F. LABORATORIES
Italy
    facebook.com/videomalattie
    vlfvideo.blogspot.com